# ENGLISH EXTRA

## Leaving Certificate Ordinary Level

A handbook to
improve your
exam grade in
**Leaving
Certificate
English**

**EDMOND BEHAN**

Published by
CJ Fallon Ltd
Ground Floor – Block B
Liffey Valley Office Campus
Dublin 22

First Edition January 2014

Welcome to *English Extra!*, a new student-focused handbook to help you to achieve the best possible result in your Leaving Certificate, English Ordinary Level examination!

Jammed full of lively sample answers, essential exam advice and key tips, **this book is designed to be used in conjunction with your textbooks and previous exam papers** to comprehensively prepare you for both Paper 1 and Paper 2.

*English Extra!* will be your companion throughout your English course, providing the extra assistance you need to reach your potential. It will help you to read, plan, time and answer your exam questions in the most efficient and effective manner.

Remember to use this book throughout the year to **maximise your performance!**

This is much more than a 'revision' book. *English Extra!* will be like your own personal tutor, as it guides you step by step through each element of the examination, showing you how to prepare effectively for each question, so that you can achieve top marks on the day. Prepare for success with *English Extra!*

Good luck!

**Edmond Behan**

Leaving Certificate English – Ordinary Level

# Contents

Leaving Certificate English – Ordinary Level

# Chapter 1

## The Exam Papers

This chapter contains the following sections. You should tick the boxes as you complete each section.

- Introduction ☐
- PAPER 1: A Detailed Breakdown with Key Approaches ☐
- PAPER 2: A Detailed Breakdown with Key Approaches ☐
- PCLM: What I Need to Know About the Marking Scheme ☐

## Introduction

Welcome to *English Extra! Leaving Certificate English – Ordinary Level*, which is full of expert advice and concise key tips to help you to achieve the best possible marks in your Leaving Certificate English exam.

Students who study the **Ordinary Level** course in English must sit two papers, for which the overall total mark is 400.

Both papers carry 200 marks.
- **Paper 1** tests your comprehending and writing skills. **Paper 2** tests your understanding of the prescribed texts on your course – the Single Text, your Comparative Study and Poetry.
- Let us begin with an overview of the exam papers and then we can take a more detailed look at each section.

## Paper 1: Overview of Layout and Mark Allocation

Total Marks:     200
Time Allowed:   2 hours 50 minutes

| Section I | Comprehending | 100 marks | |
|---|---|---|---|
| | Question A | 50 marks | To revise for this exam question see pages 13 to 70 |
| | Question B | 50 marks | To revise for this exam question see pages 71 to 113 |
| Section II | Composing | 100 marks | To revise for this exam question see pages 114 to 156 |

## Paper 2: Overview of Layout and Mark Allocation

Total Marks:     200
Time Allowed:   3 hours 20 minutes

| Section I | The Single Text | 60 marks | To revise for this exam question see pages 159 to 189 |
|---|---|---|---|
| Section II | The Comparative Study | 70 marks | To revise for this exam question see pages 190 to 212 |
| Section III | Poetry | 70 marks | |
| | Unseen Poem | 20 marks | To revise for this exam question see pages 214 to 218 |
| | Prescribed Poetry | 50 marks | To revise for this exam question see pages 218 to 226 |

# Paper 1

## A Detailed Breakdown with Key Approaches

Total Marks:      200
Time Allowed:   2 Hours 50 Minutes

Paper 1 is designed to test the **comprehending and composing abilities of students**. It consists of two main sections as follows.

## Section I: Comprehending (100 marks)

### Question A: 50 Marks

- Three texts usually appear on the exam paper, one of which may have a visual element.

To revise for this exam<br/>question, see pages<br/>**13 to 70**

- You must answer the questions on **one** of the three texts.

- Expect at least three questions on your chosen text.

- The questions instruct you to respond to the content, to the individuals referred to in the passage, and to the way that the writer described people, places and events in the passage.

- You may also be asked for a personal response to the text.

- Refer **closely** to the passage in support of your points. You may also quote from the passage, but **do not** quote whole sections or paragraphs from the text. In other words, **do not** rewrite the passage – analyse it!

- Quote only words and key phrases that are *most relevant* in supporting the point that you are making.

- Use the quote. **Explain what it shows you**, why it is important, what you learn from it and so on.

- In summary, make your point, quote from the passage, explain what the quote shows.

### Question B: 50 Marks

To revise for this exam<br/>question, see pages<br/>**71 to 113**

- Question B is a functional writing task – to write, for example, a review, talk, letter, diary, blog, feature article, newspaper report, radio/TV commentary, report on a local issue, interview, description piece, or an opinion piece.

- Make sure you know exactly what the **purpose** of your writing task is **and** for what **audience** you are writing; for example, your friends or family, school principal, graduation audience, radio audience, or readers of a teenage or school magazine. Many questions in this section tell you who your audience is – make sure you allow for this while planning your answer. There are several examples in this book that will help you to improve your functional writing skills.

- Remember, you may use any of the material/texts on the exam paper as a resource to generate ideas or approaches for your writing in Question B.

## Section II: Composing (100 marks)

To revise for this exam question, see pages

**114 to 156**

- There is usually a choice of seven composition assignments ranging from a short story or narrative, talk or speech, personal account, descriptive composition, magazine or newspaper article, series of diary entries to a serious or light-hearted opinion piece.

- Note that your composing assignment is written in **bold print** on the exam paper.

- While you will be rewarded for a creative and imaginative composition, you must also pay attention to your **use of language** and your **spelling**, **grammar** and **punctuation**. (See the section *What I Need to Know About the Marking Scheme* on page 7.)

### Special Instructions

- Both sections of the paper must be attempted.

- In Section I, Comprehending, one Question A and one Question B must be answered.

- You must answer a Question A on one text and a Question B on a **different** text. This means that you may **not** answer a Question A and a Question B on the same text.

- In Section II, Composing, you must write on **one** of the composition titles on the exam paper. Expect to find seven composition titles on the exam paper.

- Note also that the composition titles are intended to reflect your study of language in the areas of information, argument, persuasion, narration and the aesthetic use of language.

# Paper 2

## A Detailed Breakdown with Key Approaches

Total Marks:     200
Time Allowed:  3 Hours 20 Minutes

Paper 2 is designed to test the students' knowledge of, and response to, a range of texts. It consists of three main sections as follows.

## Section I: the Single Text (60 marks)

To revise for this exam
question, see pages

**159 to 189**

- In the exam, turn directly to the questions on your Single Text. Do not waste time reading any questions on the alternative Single Texts.

- Answer all of the questions on your chosen Single Text.

- **Avoid** writing a long summary of your chosen text. Focus on the **detail** required by the question instead.

- Where your opinion or evaluation is required, refer **closely** to the text in support of your points.

- The longer question (30 marks) may ask you to engage in an **imaginative** way with your Single Text. For example, you might have to imagine you are one of the characters in the text, where you have to write a letter or diary entry from that character's point of view.

- In the exam, make sure you can write out the correct **title** (and spelling) of your chosen text and the **author's name**.

- Write the name of your Single Text, and of the author here:

  - **Title** _____

  - **Author's Name** _____

## Section II: the Comparative Study (70 marks)

To revise for this exam
question, see pages

**190 to 212**

- You are required to answer **one** of four questions in this section.

- Two of the comparative modes will appear on the exam paper.

- You must answer **one** full question from mode A **or** mode B.

- The modes change each year. Make sure you know the modes to study for your exam.

- The comparative question usually asks you to discuss two texts (although three texts may be studied).

- **Do not** write 'separate essays' on each text especially where a question asks you to 'Compare and Contrast' the texts.

- Practise writing answers where you compare and contrast your texts frequently, preferably in each paragraph. 'Compare and Contrast' means you can discuss the similarities and/or differences between the texts.

- You may **not** use your Single Text as one of your comparative texts.

- Note also that you may **not** use two films in the comparative study.

- Make sure each one of your comparative texts is on the prescribed list of texts for the year of your exam.

5

● Write the names of your two/three comparative texts in the following boxes, and the writer/director of each:

| My Comparative Texts | Author/Director | Genre (Play, Novel, Film etc.) |
|---|---|---|
| ▪ _____ | _____ | _____ |
| ▪ _____ | _____ | _____ |
| ▪ _____ | _____ | _____ |

## Section III: Poetry (70 marks)

### ◉ Unseen Poem (20 marks)

● Answer the questions on the Unseen Poem. Expect at least two questions.

● You are encouraged to respond in a **personal way** to the Unseen Poem.

● However, you may also use poetic terms such as alliteration, imagery, and simile where it helps you to make your point more clearly.

● Make sure you **read the questions very carefully** before you begin to answer. This should help you to avoid the quite common pitfall of students rambling on about the poem without actually answering the question at all!

To revise for this exam question, see pages

214 to 218

### ◉ Prescribed Poetry (50 marks)

● Answer the questions on **one** of the Prescribed Poems. Expect four poems to appear in this section.

● Each of these four poems will be printed on the exam paper.

● In your answer, try to **show your understanding** of the poem.

● Avoid writing very short answers that simply make a brief statement, without reference or support, and which do not engage with the poem in any real detail.

● Every time you make a key point, use the poem – its **content** and its **language** – to support your views. There are many examples in this text to show you how to do this.

● However, just because the poem is printed on the paper, do not be tempted to write out huge chunks of the poem. It is better to quote a few phrases, perhaps a line or two from different sections of the poem that are relevant to the point that you are making.

● Some of the tasks in Question 2 may ask for **an imaginative or creative response** by suggesting, for example, that you are a character in the poem, or that you live in the setting of the poem. You might be asked to make a short video about the poem.

To revise for this exam question, see pages

218 to 226

● **Titles of Poems I Must Revise**

- _____
- _____
- _____
- _____
- _____
- _____
- _____
- _____
- _____
- _____

- _____
- _____
- _____
- _____
- _____
- _____
- _____
- _____
- _____
- _____

## Special Instructions

You must attempt the following:

● **One** question from Section I – the Single Text. Note also that the text you answer on in this section may **not** be used in your Comparative Study section.

● **One** question from Section II – the Comparative Study.

● **The questions** on the Unseen Poem from Section III – Poetry.

● The questions on **one** of the Prescribed Poems from Section III – Poetry.

# PCLM

## What I Need to Know About the Marking Scheme

*Every* assignment on your exam papers, both Paper 1 and Paper 2, is marked using the same criteria. In other words, the person marking your answers will award marks for each answer as follows.

PCLM:
Clarity of **Purpose**.
**Coherence** of Delivery.
Efficiency of **Language** Use.
Accuracy of **Mechanics**.

### P = Clarity of PURPOSE

**Focus on key terms!**

Thirty per cent of the marks for the question are awarded for **clarity of purpose**.

- This means that you must **answer the question that is asked** and not the question that you think is there, or the question that you wish was there!

- **The points you make must be relevant** to the question. Do not waffle off the point. Focus on what the question instructs you to do and nothing else.

- In terms of marks, imagine you are writing an answer to an unseen passage and the full question is worth 50 marks. Then, if 30 per cent of the marks go for **clarity of purpose**, this means that 15 marks out of the 50 for that question are awarded for following the instructions in the question.

### C = COHERENCE of Delivery

**Do not wander off the point!**

Thirty per cent of the marks for the question are awarded for **coherence of delivery**.

- This means that you must **remain focused on the question** asked over your entire answer. The answer should be well organised with each key idea developed in a paragraph of its own.

- Do not stray off the point. How can you do that? Plan your answer! You will see lots of examples in this book.

- Refer closely to the text to support your point. Then explain why you have selected a particular reference or quotation – what does it tell you about a character, or place or event and so on.

- **Use occasional quotations too but do not overdo it**, especially with texts that are printed on the exam paper – the comprehending texts, the Unseen Poem and the Prescribed Poems.

- In a 50-mark question, 15 marks may be awarded for **coherence of delivery**.

### L = Efficiency of LANGUAGE Use

**Use appropriate language to communicate clearly!**

Thirty per cent of the marks for the question are awarded for **efficiency of language use**.

- To score high marks here, you should make sure your vocabulary is suited to the task. For example, the type of vocabulary you use in writing a report on bullying for your school principal would be very different to the language that you would use in a personal diary.

● Your examiner will award you higher marks if your language is appropriate to your writing task and if you communicate clearly with your reader/audience.
A talk to a class of First Years, for example, should sound very different to a talk to a group of parents. There are many examples in this text that will help you to understand what is appropriate language.

● **Punctuation is also important.** It helps you to **communicate clearly** with your audience.

● This might seem an obvious point, but you must **remember to organise your ideas into paragraphs**. Apart from making your answer clearer to read and easier to follow, it also helps the examiner to award you marks for convincing points.

● Where possible, you should also try to **link your paragraphs together**, to almost 'stitch' your points together, in a logical way, so as to answer the question in a step-by-step manner. This is why planning your answer before you start to write is so important. Again, there are lots of examples of effective paragraphing in this book.

● Try to **include some variety in your sentences** – make some shorter, some a little longer. This simple technique adds interest for a reader.

● In a 50-mark question, 15 marks may be awarded for **language use**.

## M = Accuracy of MECHANICS

Spelling and grammar are important!

Ten per cent of the marks for the question are awarded for **accuracy of mechanics**.

● In the pressure situation of a state exam, it may be tempting to rush everything and take a careless approach towards your spelling and grammar. This is *not* a good idea.

● If you feel your spelling is weak, make sure you spell correctly some of the key words that you will use in the exam. For example, in a poetry answer, make sure you can spell commonly used words such as 'poem', 'stanza', 'poet', 'imagery', 'sound effects' and so on.

● In a 50-mark question, 5 marks may be awarded for **mechanics**.

## How PCLM Applies to the Main Sections

|  | 20-mark question | 50-mark question | 60-mark question | 70-mark question | 100-mark question |
|---|---|---|---|---|---|
|  | Unseen Poetry | Comprehending Question A; Comprehending Question B; Prescribed Poetry | The Single Text | The Comparative Study | The Composition |
| **P** (30% of marks) | 6 | 15 | 18 | 21 | 30 |
| **C** (30% of marks) | 6 | 15 | 18 | 21 | 30 |
| **L** (30% of marks) | 6 | 15 | 18 | 21 | 30 |
| **M** (10% of marks) | 2 | 5 | 6 | 7 | 10 |

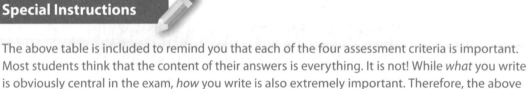

## Special Instructions

The above table is included to remind you that each of the four assessment criteria is important. Most students think that the content of their answers is everything. It is not! While *what* you write is obviously central in the exam, *how* you write is also extremely important. Therefore, the above table serves as a reminder to write as accurately and appropriately in the exam as you can. If you wish, you could write PCLM onto your exam paper first thing, in large bold letters, just to remind you on the day to **plan** your answer, keep **focused** on the question, use **paragraphs**, and be as accurate as possible in your spelling, grammar, punctuation, paragraphing and so on. These things matter too!

# Paper 1

- Paper 1, Section I – Comprehending: Question A

- Paper 1, Section I – Comprehending: Question B

- Paper 1, Section II – Composing

# Chapter 2

## Paper 1, Sec. I – Comprehending: Question A

This chapter contains the following sections. You should tick the boxes as you complete each section.

- Introduction ☐
- RPTA: Key Tips to Maximise Your Marks ☐
- The Five Language Categories ☐
- The Visual Text ☐
- Language Categories ☐
- Key Exam Tips ☐
- Your Last Minute Revision! ☐

## Introduction

In Section I, Comprehending: Question A, you will learn how to read and understand the exam questions thoroughly, and how to construct an answer plan that addresses the key terms in each question.

These are skills that you must practise regularly because misreading or misunderstanding a question can be damaging. By following the guidelines in this chapter, you will be able to clearly identify the essence of each question in the exam, so that you know exactly what is expected from you before you begin writing your answer.

One of the key features of every effective answer is preparation. Your answer plan, therefore, is a hugely important examination tool that will guide your response and ensure it is focused and coherent throughout. There are effective sample answer plans in this section including some really practical planning tips from students who have already been through the exam process and succeeded.

The guidelines in the chapter emphasise the importance of writing with a clear purpose for a particular audience, while the sample answers illustrate good practice in introducing, paragraphing, elaborating, supporting and concluding your points. You will find several examples of excellent answers to comprehending questions in addition to an analysis of the various types of questions you may expect on the exam paper.

Finally, the Study Cards provide concise notes and easy reference on the five language categories to help you to effectively read – and write – the languages of information, narration, argument, persuasion and, also, aesthetic language.

# RPTA

## Key Tips to Maximise your Marks

RPTA:
Read
Plan
Time
Answer

### Starting Out – RPTA

 **Key Tip 1: READ the Question Correctly**

One of the most important things you can do in your exam is to read each question correctly. Far too many students get low marks in their answers, not because they cannot answer the question but because they answer the 'wrong' question. In other words, they do not answer what is asked.

> **HINT**
>
> Before deciding on your Question A text, make sure that you read the Question Bs as well. Mark what you think might be your strongest Question B. Then consider answering Question A on either one of the other two remaining Comprehending texts on the paper.

If your answer is irrelevant, you will lose a lot of marks!

● Therefore, read each question at least three times, then <u>underline</u> or **highlight** the key terms in that question.

**Key Tip 2: PLAN Your Answer**

- OK, so you have read the question and identified what you have to do. But don't start writing an answer just yet! Allow a few minutes to make a rough draft or plan of the keypoints that you want to make, then develop these points in your written answer.

> Poor points don't make good answers!

- No matter how good a writer you are, if the points you make are not relevant or significant, your grade will be low. To improve, make sure you plan some strong, relevant, key points before you start writing paragraphs.

 **Key Tip 3: TIME your Answer**

Time Allowed (Paper 1):
2 Hours 50 Minutes

- Allow **10 minutes** at the beginning of the exam to familiarise yourself with the paper *before* you write anything.

 **Suggested Time for Each Section**

**Section I: Comprehending (100 marks)**

Suggested Time:
1 Hour 25 Minutes

- Question A (50 marks) approximately 50 minutes – includes reading time and planning time.
- Question B (50 marks) approximately 35 minutes – includes planning time.

**Section II: Composing (100 marks)**

Suggested Time:
1 Hour 15 Minutes

- Allow at least 75 minutes for your composition. Includes planning time and time to read over your composition to check for accuracy in layout, paragraphing, spelling, grammar and so on.

| Paper 1 | |
|---|---|
| **SECTION** | **TIME** |
| I   Comprehending Question A | 50 mins |
| I   Comprehending Question B | 35 mins |
| II  Composing | 75 mins |
| | **160 mins** |
| + reading paper and checking at end of exam | 10 mins |
| | **170 mins** |

**Key Tip 4: ANSWER the Question Asked**

● Just before you begin to write your full answer, look once again at the question, then at your plan. If you think that your plan is not directly answering **each** key term or instruction in the question, you have time to make slight changes **now**.

● Better to adjust things now than to have to cross out a complete page of an answer later.

● When you are happy that your plan is relevant, you can be confident that you have prepared a solid foundation for your answer. Check again your time allowance for the question, and then begin.

# The Five Language Categories

## 1. THE LANGUAGE OF INFORMATION

### Study Card No.1: The Language of Information

● The language of information is usually **easy to understand** by its intended audience.

● The information is **written clearly** to avoid confusion.

● The information is **relevant** and carefully selected by the writer to meet a specific purpose: to inform, to educate, to clarify, to warn, to show, to entertain, etc.

● The information/facts may come from a report, from people's own experiences, from a description of events that have occurred and so on.

● Illustrations or photographs may be included with the information to make it easier to follow, and more memorable.

● Many informative texts **present facts** that answer the 5W + H questions for the reader – *who, what, why, when, where* and *how*.

● Many informative texts have a **neutral tone**. Occasionally, however, a writer may create a more subjective tone. This occurs when a writer includes some opinions, and may show feelings such as admiration, anger, sadness, disappointment or hope.

## From the Exam Papers

Read and analyse the informative Text 1 passage below (source: Leaving Certificate, Ordinary Level, Paper 1, 2010). Try to identify examples of some of the features of informative texts. Say why a particular feature is being used or what it adds to the passage.

Finally, read the exam questions on the passage carefully. Underline or highlight the key terms. Make a plan and then answer the three questions. Compare your answer with the sample answers given.

> Don't forget to read the information (the foreword) at the top of the passage. It may signpost what the passage is about (its **content**) and tell you why the passage was written (its **purpose**).

> The passage begins with biographical **information** on Martin Strel. Note how the writer uses words to create a **positive impression** of Strel: 'greatest', 'famously', 'very strong', 'broke the record'.

> The description of the Amazon river is very informative: 'most dangerous river in the world', 'home to the bull shark', and 'long poisonous snakes can appear from nowhere'. This information sets out very clearly the enormous challenges that faced Martin Strel. This gives the reader the impression that Strel was a very brave person.

### SECTION I
### COMPREHENDING (100 marks)
### TEXT I
### DANGEROUS CHALLENGES

**Martin Strel and Sophie Collett are world-class athletes who take part in extreme sports at the highest level. The following passages tell us a little about their adventures.**

**Martin Strel**, from Slovenia, is the greatest long-distance swimmer the world has known. He famously completed a 3,278 mile swim of the Amazon. Strel is about six feet tall and very strong. He has a wrestler's neck and his body is coated with fat and muscle. When compared to a fit, toned Olympic swimmer he barely looks like an athlete at all. He swam the English Channel, the Paraná in Argentina and the Yangtze River in China. He also broke the record for the longest continuous swim, non-stop 313 miles, in the Danube in Germany.

The most dangerous river in the world, the Amazon, was his next challenge. He started in a tropical rain storm. The flooding was the worst in the Amazon area for 100 years.

There are sharks in the Amazon. It is home to the bull shark, widely believed to have killed more humans than any other shark species. There are also piranhas which have been described as the "most aggressive and savage of all aquatic animals". There are stingrays and anacondas lurking in the shallows. Long poisonous snakes can appear from nowhere while giant catfish have been known to swallow dogs and children. Those in the boats accompanying Strel could see him mouthing words. He was talking to the fish, telling them he was their friend.

He tried not to look down and instead of thinking of 'monster' creatures below him he would think of his family.

Tarantulas and scorpions dropped off trees and floated down on leaves. Wasp stings made his head hum for days. Large black birds flew down to peck at his face. He had to wear a pillowcase over his head with slits for eyes and mouth because he had second-degree burns from the sun. Strel, like all marathon swimmers, certainly is a breed apart.

**Sophie Collett** describes her Jungle Marathon experience as the "toughest event in the world". "The Jungle Marathon is 125 miles and is run over seven days through the Amazon rainforest in Brazil. The race is broken down into six stages. Once I got started it became clear that the biggest hazard facing me wasn't the animals. It was the plants and the landscape. I had to climb over many fallen trees and wade through lots of swamp.

When I went there I had a massive fear of spiders, but of course these creatures are all over the place in the jungle. On one of the stages, at night, I found myself crawling under a log that clearly harboured an awful lot of insects. But there was no question of getting freaked out. I was concentrating so hard on the race. I just got on with it.

Page 2 of 12

Finally, the writer describes the hardship endured by Strel. Being brave did not mean there was no pain. In fact, the passage tells us that Strel suffered from several injuries on his adventure: 'Wasp stings made his head hum for days. Large black birds flew down to peck at his face', and 'he had second-degree burns from the sun'. We can see from the words in the passage, that Strel is admired by the writer as he is described as being 'a breed apart'. The writer, therefore, gives information, but also includes a **personal viewpoint** in the text. The tone is not neutral – it is subjective.

I had to carry my own food and camping equipment. This included large quantities of energy drinks, freeze-dried food, plus a change of running clothes, all packed into a 30 litre rucksack. By the end of the race my arms, legs and stomach were completely shredded.

We faced the danger of heat exhaustion every day. The temperature regularly reached 30°C. For most of us, the second last stage was the worst: 54 miles of tortuous hills, jungle, two water crossings and hot, sandy ground to finish. To top it all off, I picked up a tummy bug from swallowing water when I was wading through a swamp.

I was just running along being sick in the dark. There was no one around. It felt like the stage was never going to end. Twenty-three hours later I reached the finish line.

But I was also a little sad that it was over. I loved the bond with the other runners. At times like that you make friends really quickly. It truly was my toughest challenge and finishing it gave me a great sense of achievement."

**(i) Three reasons** why Amazon is terrifying and **dangerous**. Explain, giving support from text (reference and/or quotation).

**(ii)** Agree/disagree that Strel and Collette are **remarkable**. Give three reasons, based on the information in the passage.

**(iii)** Give three or four reasons **why you think people take risks** in dangerous sporting/adventure activities. Refer to passage and/or to your own experience for support.

**N.B.  Candidates may NOT answer Question A and Question B on the same text.**

**Questions A and B carry 50 marks each.**

**Question A**

(i)  Based on your reading of the passage, give **three** reasons why you think the Amazon River is described as terrifying and dangerous.  Explain your answer with reference to the text. (15)

(ii)  Martin Strel and Sophie Collett are both remarkable people.  From what you have read about them in the above texts would you agree with this statement?  Give reasons for your answer. (15)

(iii)  Both Strel and Collett took many risks in the course of their activities. In your opinion, what makes people want to undertake such dangerous activities?  Give reasons for your answer. (20)

**Question B.**

People need to be motivated in order to face a challenge.
Imagine your class is considering undertaking a 10 kilometre cross-country run for a charity of your choice.  Write a short talk to inspire them to take up this challenge. (50)

## SAMPLE EXAM QUESTION

### Question A

(i)   Based on your reading of the passage, give three reasons why you think the Amazon River is described as terrifying and dangerous. Explain your answer with reference to the text. (15)

## ◉ Student's Answer Plan

● Amazon – home to the bull shark.

● Waters infested with piranha fish – 'aggressive and savage'.

● Other dangerous 'monster' fish include stingrays and giant catfish.

## ◉ Sample Answer to Question A (i)

In this passage, the Amazon River is described as being both terrifying and dangerous for several reasons. Firstly, the Amazon is the habitat of one of the deadliest sharks on our planet, namely the bull shark. This shark is reputedly the greatest threat to humans of all shark species and would, therefore, pose a real threat to Martin Strel's safety.

Secondly, the river is also home to the 'most aggressive and savage of all aquatic animals', the piranha fish. I imagine that an attack by a shoal of piranhas would be almost impossible to predict, it would occur almost instantaneously and would undoubtedly end up being fatal. These facts alone must be frightening to people like Martin Strel.

Finally, the river is also home to several other 'monsters' and potentially lethal animals including stingrays, anacondas, poisonous snakes and giant catfish. Understandably, such animals make the river not only dangerous to human life, but also terrifying to adventurers and explorers alike. In addition, when you consider that the river is at least 3,278 miles long, the chance of being attacked by one or more of these creatures may be quite high and certainly explains why the river is described as being both dangerous and terrifying.

### Answering Techniques

● Begin by rephrasing the question as a statement. This is a useful technique to keep your points focused and relevant to the question.

● Introduce each new point separately. This answer uses 'Firstly', 'Secondly' and 'Finally'. Use paragraphs.

● Support each key point by making reference to the passage.

19

- Take relevant quotations from the passage without overdoing it.

- Explain why the reference/quotation taken from the passage is important or interesting.

- Give three reasons as instructed and indicate clearly when you are moving on to each new point.

- Use your own words to develop the three points in the plan and explain your reasons fully.

- Make your points clearly. Take care with your spelling, punctuation, grammar and paragraphing.

**Question A**

(ii)  Martin Strel and Sophie Collett are both remarkable people. From what you have read about them in the above texts would you agree with this statement? Give reasons for your answer. (15)

## ◎ Student's Answer Plan

**Strel**

- 3,278-mile swim – extreme conditions.

- Swam other rivers.

- World record breaker.

- Huge determination – will power.

- Self-belief incredible – a 'breed apart'.

**Collett**

- 125-mile jungle marathon.

- Plants and animals increased difficulty of challenge.

- Overcame her fear of spiders.

- No question of freaking out – complete concentration on task before her.

- Body 'shredded', yet could still endure temperatures of 30+ degrees – heat exhaustion.

- Variety of terrain: 'tortuous hills'.

- Sick in the dark' – yet continued with the race to the finish line.

**Sample Answer to Question A (ii)**

Having read the extract, I am convinced that Martin Strel and Sophie Collett are remarkable people. They have both achieved incredible feats, against the odds, in difficult and hostile environments.

Martin Strel is certainly a remarkable man. According to the passage, he has completed a series of extraordinary adventures such as swimming the English Channel, the Paraná in Argentina and the Yangtze River in China. He has also broken the world record for swimming 313 miles non-stop in the River Danube. However, Strel's achievement that really impressed me was his 3,278 mile swim of the Amazon River. This was no leisurely swim, but a massive challenge, where dangerous and life-threatening animals lurked at every bend in the river. To complete this challenge demands huge reserves of stamina, mental strength and sheer determination. That Strel could drive himself to achieve this task, while surviving the bull sharks and piranhas of the murky depths of the Amazon, makes him, in my opinion, a remarkable person, and a 'breed apart'.

Equally remarkable for her adventures is Sophie Collett. That she completed a 125-mile marathon does, in my view, qualify her to be seen as a remarkable person. Moreover, Collett also had to battle through swamps and over fallen trees, sapping her energy. She also overcame her fear of spiders, when her determination meant 'there was no question of getting freaked out'. I admire the way that she 'just got on with it'. I was also impressed by her ability to keep going despite everything: her 'shredded' body, being 'sick in the dark' and the 'tortuous hills' that met her along the way.

Based on the information in the passage, I would strongly agree with the statement that Martin Strel and Sophie Collett are both remarkable people.

### Answering Techniques

- The question asks for your own opinion. You can agree or disagree that Strel and Collett are remarkable. Begin by stating whether you agree or disagree with the statement.

- Remember, the question asks if both athletes are remarkable, so discuss each in turn.

- Explain your opinion. Keep in mind why you think that the athletes are remarkable. You must not only say that they are/are not remarkable, but, more importantly, you must explain *why* you think so. After all, the question does say to give reasons for your answer.

- **Use your own words** when explaining your points. The best approach is to make your point. Next, include reference/quotation from the passage that illustrates or supports your point. Finally, in your own words, discuss what the reference/quotation tells you about Strel or Collett.

- Make a brief concluding statement.

**Question A**

(iii) Both Strel and Collett took many risks in the course of their activities. In your opinion, what makes people want to undertake such dangerous activities? Give reasons for your answer. (20)

## Student's Answer Plan

**Tick the points that you will develop in your answer.**

- Bond with other like-minded athletes. ☐

- Huge sense of achievement. ☐

- The fame. ☐

- Increases determination to face up to personal fears. ☐

**Your own points**

- _____

- _____

- _____

## Practise Your Answering Skills

**Sample Answer to Question A (iii)**

Write your own answer to this question here.

_____

_____

_____

_____

_____

_____

## 2. THE LANGUAGE OF NARRATION

**Study Card No.2:** The Language of Narration

**The Features**

- First and foremost, narrative language tells a story.
- Most texts with narrative language have a strong sense of a beginning, a middle and an ending.
- The **setting** (time and place), the **characters** (real or imaginary), and the **action** are all important parts of a successful narrative.
- Language of narration is frequently **descriptive**. Note the importance of well-chosen verbs and adjectives that build a strong sense of place and of action.
- Note also the **variety of sentences** in a narrative passage – some sentences are short, some longer – this makes writing more lively and dramatic and more interesting to read.
- Events in a narrative are often told by a first-person or third-person narrator.
- Many narratives include moments of **insight**. Some include observations, or longer reflections by the writer, narrator or characters on the experience being described.
- Effective narratives tell us about interesting, realistic and even recognisable characters placed in unusual, challenging, humorous or difficult situations.
- Dialogue in narratives is sometimes used to develop the plot (move the story forward), to dramatise relationships between characters, or create a certain atmosphere (happiness, fear, anger, etc.).
- Note that fictional narratives include short stories, novels, etc., while non-fictional narratives include news stories, autobiographies, diaries, travel writing, etc.

## From the Exam Papers

Read and analyse the narrative passage indicated below (source: Leaving Certificate, Ordinary Level, Paper 1, 2010). Identify examples of some of the features of narrative texts mentioned on Study Card No. 2. Try to say why a particular feature is being used or what it adds to the passage. Finally, read the exam questions on the passage carefully. Underline or highlight the key terms. Make a plan and then answer the three questions. Compare your answers with the sample answers.

Don't forget to read the information, including the title, at the top of the passage. This **foreword**, tells us the who, what, why, when, where and how. It also refers to the episode as being 'frightening'. This information will help you to **read the passage in context** and, therefore, understand it more easily.

The illustration helps to create a clear visual picture of the action.

Severin tells the story in the order in which it actually occurred: the beginning, middle and end.

**Vivid description** is often a feature of narrative texts.

**Setting**, **characters** and **action** all combine to make this part of the story very dramatic and exciting.

### TEXT 2
### ACROSS THE ATLANTIC IN A LEATHER BOAT

Explorer and author Tim Severin sailed across the Atlantic in 1977. He used a leather-clad boat in order to test the legend that an Irish monk named Brendan had completed the same voyage in the sixth century. The following edited extract from Severin's book, *The Brendan Voyage*, tells of a frightening episode that occurred during the journey.

1. Our craft looked like a floating banana: long and slim, curved at the ends. No boat quite like her had been afloat for the past thousand years or so. She was made from forty-nine ox hides stitched together to form a patchwork quilt and stretched over a wooden frame. It was this thin skin, only a quarter of an inch thick, that now stood between us and the fury of the Atlantic. In such a gale even a modern yacht would have been hard pressed to hold up against the weather. For us, in a boat of ancient design, there was no choice but to do our best to stay afloat while *Brendan* tobogganed down the waves.

2. Our vessel was essentially an open boat swept by the wind and spray. There was a tent with room for three men to lie down, head to tail, like sardines. But here we also had to find space for clothes, the camera, other equipment and sleeping bags. Whenever a wave broke it had the nasty habit of sweeping forward and dropping like a thick dollop of water right into our shelter. There was another small tent, not much bigger than a good sized kennel. There the other crew members were expected to sleep but the leaks were even worse. Each time a wave broke it sent a fountain of cold water squirting up under the tent flap and drenched the men.

3. I looked at my crew and wondered if they realised how serious the situation was. George was one of the best sailors I knew. He was the sailing master, the man responsible for getting the very best performance from the boat under sail. Rolf was from Norway and spent his summers exploring his country's coastline in a massive sailing boat. Peter, our cameraman, worried me. He had damaged muscles from rowing *Brendan*. His face had a grey look as he was tossed around with the constant motion of the boat. Arthur was the youngest member of the crew and he was laid low by seasickness. I had rarely seen anyone so miserable.

4. Night came. A dirty, black night with rain and very bad visibility. Suddenly, out of the darkness less than a hundred yards away and with all her lights blazing, there was a large factory ship heading straight in our direction. Peter struggled trying to steer the boat clear.
"Light a white flare!" I yelled at Peter. "Light a flare."
"What about shining a torch on the sails?" asked Rolf.
"No good," I shouted above the howling wind. "Our sail isn't big enough to work as a light reflector. Besides it's made of leather and won't reflect the light properly."

Page 4 of 12

The very short sentence, 'Night came' helps to create a tense atmosphere.

This is a **first-person narrative**. Tim Severin is telling this story from experience, which makes it more real and more dramatic.

(i) The question asks for **your** opinion. Identify **three** difficulties, then **explain** why you have chosen each one. Refer to and quote **from the text** to support your reasons.

(ii) Focus on paragraphs 4 and 5 only. Agree or disagree that the writer shows the atmosphere of both **tension** and **fear**. Select words and phrases and suggest how they create atmosphere.

(iii) Again, the question asks for your opinion. State if you think Severin and his crew were brave or foolish or both. Refer closely to evidence in the passage in support of your points.

**5.** Someone had found a white flare but fingers were too cold and stiff to unwrap the tape and light it. Peter struggled trying to turn *Brendan* away but the wind had locked us on what seemed to be a collision course. Then the factory trawler's black bulk slid past us so close that we could make out the welding on the steel plates that towered over us. The lights from her portholes swept over us. We stood looking up at this giant of the sea. She was so close we could reach out and touch her.

**N.B.** Candidates may NOT answer Question A and Question B on the same text.

Questions A and B carry 50 marks each.

**Question A**

(i) In your opinion, what were the **three** greatest difficulties faced by Tim Severin and his crew? Explain your answer with reference to the text. (15)

(ii) In paragraphs 4 and 5 how does Tim Severin convey the atmosphere of tension and fear on *Brendan* as the huge factory ship came towards them? (15)

(iii) From your reading of the passage do you think Tim Severin and his crew were brave or foolish or both to undertake their voyage? Give reasons for your answer. (20)

**Question B**

A competition has been announced to select crew members for a new *Brendan* voyage. In approximately 250 words explain to Tim Severin why you should be chosen as a crew member for this voyage. (50)

## SAMPLE EXAM QUESTION

### Question A

(i) In your opinion, what were the **three** greatest difficulties faced by Tim Severin and his crew? Explain your answer with reference to the text. (15)

## ◉ Student's Answer Plan

● Boat of ancient design – 'thin skin'.

● Constant drenching, dampness, sickness – 'fountain of cold water . . . drenched the men'.

● Danger of collision with other, larger vessels – 'a large factory ship heading straight in our direction'.

26

## ◉ Sample Answer to Question A (i)

From my reading of the passage, I think Tim Severin and his crew faced several difficulties.

One of the greatest difficulties was the fact that the boat on which they sailed across the Atlantic was built to a design over a thousand years old. Severin had to survive the furious Atlantic waves floating on a 'thin skin, only a quarter of an inch thick'. Had Severin crossed the ocean in a modern, fully equipped vessel with the latest safety features, his difficulties in simply 'staying afloat' might have been far less pressing.

Another difficulty faced by the crew was the endless sweeping of waves over the boat, resulting in wet, damp and leaking tents where the men were expected to sleep. The fact that they were cold, tired and damp would only have added to the stress and exhaustion experienced by the sailors, adding to the difficulty of their challenge.

A third difficulty that they faced involved navigation. Without the benefit of modern radar, the first warning that they got of an approaching vessel was when it was 'less than a hundred yards away'. Severin's leather boat, *Brendan*, would be no match for large, factory ships that loomed out of the eerie darkness. Were it not for sheer luck, the black 'steel plates' of such a 'giant of the sea' would have crushed the *Brendan* in an instant, while her crew may have drowned or, at best, been seriously injured.

The three greatest difficulties, therefore, faced by Severin and his crew were the flimsy structure of their sailing boat, the endless drenching by the cold sea, and the danger of colliding with larger vessels.

### Answering Techniques

- Begin by rephrasing the question as a statement.
- Use paragraphs: one paragraph for each key point.
- Support the key point by making reference to/quoting from the passage.
- Develop the paragraph/the point by explaining why the reference/quotation taken from the passage is important or interesting.
- Give three of the greatest difficulties and clearly indicate when you are moving on to each new point.
- Refer back to your plan before you begin each paragraph to help you to keep focused on your key point.
- Summarise briefly your key points in the conclusion.

## Question A

(ii)  In paragraphs 4 and 5, how does Tim Severin convey the atmosphere of tension and fear on Brendan as the huge factory ship came towards them? (15)

## ◉ Student's Answer Plan

- Language and imagery create mood/atmosphere.
- Description of factory ship – 'black bulk' – atmosphere of fear.
- Dialogue creates tension.
- Atmosphere created by word choice, appeals to senses; vivid adjectives, verbs, etc.

## ◉ Sample Answer to Question A (ii)

In paragraphs 4 and 5, Tim Severin conveys an atmosphere of tension and fear as the factory ship appeared out of the darkness.

Severin creates tension with a careful choice of vocabulary to create a dramatic setting. Paragraph 4 begins with a very pithy sentence: 'Night came'. Using adjectives, he then graphically describes the night as 'a dirty, black night with rain and very bad visibility'. This creates a sense of foreboding in the reader, and the choice of the phrase 'very bad visibility' added to the tension and gave me the impression that something unexpected was about to happen. In addition, the reference to the 'howling wind' helps to set the scene for an imminent disaster.

The writer's description of the sudden appearance of the factory ship in paragraph 4 also creates an atmosphere of tension and fear. Severin paints a vivid picture of a 'giant of the sea' using verbs and adjectives that make it fearful and menacing, while also heightening the tension. For example, 'all her lights were blazing' as she appeared out of the darkness. She is pictured as a 'black bulk', with 'steel plates that towered' over the Brendan. From these descriptions, I could understand why Severin and his crew would have been terrified by the approach of such a powerful factory ship.

Finally, Severin cleverly includes dialogue and descriptions of action in the passage. The desperate calls of the crew to 'Light a white flare' and their frantic efforts to prevent a collision are very gripping. The tension builds further in paragraph 5, when Severin describes how Peter 'struggled trying to turn the Brendan'. Despite the crew's frantic efforts, Severin remarks that the 'wind had locked us on what seemed to be a collision course'. At this point, a collision seems inevitable as the tension and fear reach a climax.

It is clear, therefore, that careful word selection, variety in sentence structure and the use of dialogue and vivid description are all used effectively by Tim Severin to create tension and fear in the passage.

## Answering Techniques

- Begin with your opening statement.

- Avoid padding with irrelevant points. **Plan out your points beforehand**. This should prevent you from merely summarising the paragraphs. The question is looking for analysis, not summary.

- Only refer to the relevant paragraphs, 4 and 5.

- Once you make your point, support it. Notice how in the above answer, the writer does not just write down quotations but discusses them and indicates what they show or suggest.

- Select appropriate words and phrases that you think create the atmosphere of tension/fear. Refer to these words or quote them, then explain how they create the atmosphere.

- In each paragraph, refer back to the question to show that you focused on its key terms.

- Finish with a brief concluding statement.

### Question A

(iii) From your reading of the passage do you think Tim Severin and his crew were brave or foolish or both to undertake their voyage? (20)

## ◎ Student's Answer Plan

**Tick the points that you will develop in your answer.**

**BRAVE**

- Using a vessel not used for over a thousand years. ☐

- The Atlantic could be a furious sea. ☐

- Severin describes the situation they were in as 'serious'. ☐

- Passionate about sailing – despite the dangers,
  they recreated the basic conditions of a sixth-century boat. ☐

### And/or

**FOOLISH**

- An open boat 'swept by wind and spray' – seasickness,
  'miserable' crew. ☐

- Sleeping quarters very poor – no bigger than a kennel. ☐

- Risking their lives to 'test a legend' – get their priorities right. ☐

- Boat had to be rowed – no power engine. ☐

- Choice of crew – some inexperienced sailors/cameraman. ☐

**Your own points**

- _____
- _____
- _____

## Practise Your Answering Skills

### Sample Answer to Question A (iii)

Write your own answer to this question here.

_____
_____
_____
_____
_____
_____
_____
_____
_____
_____
_____
_____
_____
_____
_____
_____
_____
_____
_____
_____
_____
_____

## 3. THE LANGUAGE OF PERSUASION

### Study Card No.3: The Language of Persuasion

### The Features

- Persuasive writing may try to **influence** a reader's beliefs, or opinions or feelings. Sometimes, it may hope to change a person's behaviour.

- Persuasive language **makes a direct appeal to people's emotion**s. It does not need to focus on what is factual information.

- However, persuasive texts may include examples of information (facts), argument (logical points and conclusions), narration (anecdote), aesthetic language (imagery) and persuasion.

- **Rhetorical questions**, **repetition**, and **quotations** are frequently used to make a point more persuasive.

- **Humour** can be used to emphasise a point in a memorable way. It may also lessen our resistance to a point and it may help to encourage the audience to side with the text, speaker or writer.

- **Flattery** can be an effective way to coax an audience to consider your point. 'You are all sensible, well-balanced students sitting here in assembly today. So, I'm sure you can all see that . . . .'

- **Personal anecdotes** are another effective way of drawing an audience into a text so that their emotions can be manipulated.

- The use of **personal pronouns**, 'I, you, we', engages an audience and creates a personal tone.

- Persuasive texts can include **superlatives**, either positive superlatives (e.g. 'greatest', 'brightest', 'bravest'), or negative superlatives (e.g. 'darkest', 'worst', 'craziest'). These show us the writer's attitude in a text.

- **Comparatives** might also be used (e.g. 'better', 'richer', 'faster') to highlight differences between things.

## From the Exam Papers

Read and analyse the persuasive passage indicated below (source: Language of Persuasion in the Leaving Certificate, Ordinary Level, Paper 1, 2005). Identify examples of some of the features mentioned on Study Card No. 3. Try to say why a particular feature is being used or what it adds to the passage. Finally, read the exam questions on the passage carefully. Underline or highlight the key terms. Make a plan and then answer the three questions. Compare your answers with the sample answers.

This passage includes an interesting **combination of information and persuasion**. While the young people give information on freedom, they also explain their opinions, in an attempt to persuade us that what they say is interesting and valid.

Note the **emotive phrase**, 'for fear of being arrested or killed'. This is very persuasive and few would disagree with this point. It convinces us that 'this is not the way people should live in the world today'. Maria's response shows a strong sense of justice, of what is right and wrong.

The use of **aesthetic language** is certainly effective and makes this idea of freedom very appealing.

This person draws the audience on to her side, ('Of course everyone is an individual.') before explaining why 'not many' people want to express their individuality. Are her points facts or opinions? Do you agree with her points?

Rebecca's response shows her strong sense of self-interest.

---

## SECTION I
## COMPREHENDING (100 marks)

### TEXT I

#### What Freedom means to me...

Here is a selection from the responses made by a group of young people to the question "What does freedom mean to you?"

1. When I think of freedom, I think of all those people who are not free and how lucky I am to be able to feel safe to walk down the street or get the bus to college. I think of those in areas of conflict and how every day they are taking their lives into their hands just by going to get the groceries. I also see those who are not allowed to voice their opinions for fear of being arrested or killed. This is not the way people should live in the world today. Each person should have at least the basic freedoms: freedom from fear, freedom from poverty, and freedom to choose the life he or she wants to lead.

Maria, 21

2.  When I hear the word freedom I think of not being restricted, not having to worry about anything. I feel that freedom is a state of mind, a place inside your head where everything is calm and relaxed. When I think of freedom, I think of open green fields and bright sea-spray on a sunny day. Freedom is how I feel when I go fishing on the mountain lake. I love the soothing sound of the water against the boat, the clear blue sky, and me at peace with myself. It's an inward state like being on The Lake Isle of Inisfree!

Jason, 20

3.  It's being allowed to do what I want when I want. It's not being told I have to wear this or that but being allowed to wear what I want when I want. It's not being held back from the things I like to do. It's being able to say what I think. It's being left alone not having anyone looking over my shoulder all the time. And then there's the phone! Mobile topups cost me a fortune so I need to use the house phone a lot. Freedom would be my own phone in my own room.

Rebecca, 13

4.  To me freedom is having the choice to be an individual. Of course everyone *is* an individual. However, each person has the choice as to whether or not they want to express their individuality. Unfortunately not many people want to express it, they are quite happy to follow the crowd. They can't bear the thought of not being accepted if they think, look, or act differently. I decided from a very early age to be myself and I am very lucky to have a group of friends who don't follow the crowd. They are just themselves too. We wear what we like and listen to what we like whether it's "in" or not. In fact most of the time we get to do as we choose.

Saki, 17

Page 2 of 8

Mike begins with a general statement but **he does not rely on facts to support his point. He includes several opinions**, with which some readers might disagree. Does he use rhetorical questions effectively? Or do you think his tone undermines (weakens) his point? Do you think he talks down to the audience?

5. There is no such thing as freedom. People only think they are free – it's an illusion. So you are free to buy what you want? Yes? But they only make the things they want you to buy. Take the music industry. Unless a band is going to make a fortune for the label, then they don't get a chance of a recording contract. In that way so much good music never gets heard. So you have a vote? Well isn't that great! When you look at the parties and their different policies, beware, because when they get into government they never seem to change the way that wealth is shared out. The rich keep getting richer and the poor struggle. Freedom? It's a dream.

Mike, 23

**N.B. Candidates may NOT answer Question A and Question B on the same text.**

**Questions A and B carry 50 marks each.**

**Question A**

(i) You only discuss **one** of the five views ('the closest'). Select carefully. Choose a view that you really do agree with or a view that you would be able to write about most successfully.

(i) Which of the 5 views of freedom given above is closest to your own view? Give reasons for your answer. (15)

(ii) Which view of freedom is least like your view? Give reasons for your answer. (15)

(ii) In this question, you take one view that you find very different to your own. Again, the question instructs you to give reasons. Three reasons would be adequate.

(iii) Do you think that the age of the writer has an influence on the way he or she expresses his or her opinion? Give reasons. Refer to **two** of the responses in your answer. (20)

**Question B**

**Greater Freedom for Students**

Write a report to your school principal suggesting ways in which more freedom could be given to senior students in your school. (50)

(iii) Read this question very carefully. It does **not** ask you to discuss how a person's age influences what they say. It asks you to discuss how a person's age influences **how** they say it – the way that they use language, construct sentences, the examples they use, etc. Use two contrasting responses from the passage to support your points.

Page 3 of 8 ➡

## SAMPLE EXAM QUESTION

### Question A

(i)  Which of the 5 views of freedom given above is closest to your own view?
Give reasons for your answer. (15)

## ◉ Student's Answer Plan

● Maria – freedom to express yourself, freedom from poverty, fear.

● Freedom to express views in relationships – healthy.

● Freedom of movement – Ireland and the EU.

● Poverty holds back people – they can't chase their dreams or make them happen.

## ◉ Sample Answer to Question A (i)

Maria's view in the first paragraph in the passage closely reflects my own view on freedom.

Briefly, Maria feels that freedom is the ability to go about your daily activities without fear or harassment. She believes that freedom is being able to express yourself, to 'voice your opinions'. She also states that freedom from poverty is central to her understanding of what freedom means.

I agree with many of these views. Like Maria, I think that freedom should be about freedom of choice and freedom of movement. In our relationships, with family and friends, with our communities, and with our governments, each individual should feel free to express a personal opinion on a wide range of issues. To be denied the opportunity to share your viewpoints is undemocratic and it imprisons your mind. As Maria said, 'This is not the way people should live in the world today'.

Similarly, people who are denied freedom of movement have their bodies imprisoned. I firmly believe that all law-abiding citizens should be permitted free movement, without intimidation or threat. We see how important this has become to an enlarged EU where thousands of foreign nationals moved to Ireland recently. This freedom of movement has benefited our country.

Finally, I agree strongly with Maria that freedom from poverty is extremely important. The shackles of extreme poverty have held back millions of people in the Third World. For decades, young and old alike have seen their dreams of a better life trampled on beneath the heavy burden of poverty. Closer to home, poverty can severely hinder people's chances of further education, thus limiting their expectations and preventing them from pursuing, in Maria's words, 'the life he or she wants to lead'.

## Answering Techniques

- **Identify the view** that is closest to your own view.

- Outline that view briefly – now you have something to work on.

- **Arrange your key points into paragraphs** and make your answer more coherent by using words and phrases such as 'Similarly' and 'Finally'.

- In developing your points, you may **refer to your own knowledge**, experience and perspectives on the issue.

- Always refer back to your plan before you begin each paragraph to help you to remain focused on your key point.

- Take each key point of Maria's view and explain why it is close to your own view.

### Question A

(ii)  Which view of freedom is least like your view? Give reasons for your answer. (15)

## Student's Answer Plan

- View 5 – Mike – 'no such thing as freedom'.

- Successful music industry means more choice not less.

- Right to vote is much prized. Elections have brought results.

- Mike must believe there is some sort of utopia out there!

## Sample Answer to Question A (ii)

In the passage, the view of freedom that is least like my own would have to be Mike's view in paragraph 5.

Mike begins by stating very bluntly that 'there is no such thing as freedom'. He suggests that freedom is 'an illusion' and a 'dream'. He believes that we are being controlled by big business and big government. While I respect Mike's opinions, I would disagree strongly with his views, which I think are quite narrow-minded.

To me, it is somewhat extreme to suggest that there is no such thing as freedom. Mike seems to think that when we download a song from the internet that we are only doing it because the music industry will make money from it. But surely, that is the point – if the music industry wasn't making money, there would be no music to choose from! It is exactly because the music industry is profitable that we can download thousands of songs from the internet, in one day if we wish! I don't have to buy them; I am, however, free to choose the songs that I want to buy, because I like them! Now if that is not freedom of choice, I don't know what is!

> Mike also thinks that voting in elections is a waste of time and effort. I find this opinion somewhat insulting. Voting in elections has produced some spectacular victories on this island. European treaties have been passed, and elected politicians have brought peace to Northern Ireland. In addition, people have dedicated their lives to securing a vote in democratic elections. How else can the voice of the people be heard? It's ironic that while Mike thinks freedom is an illusion he obviously believes in the ultimate illusion – utopia!

**Answering Techniques**

- **Identify the view** that is closest to your own view.

- Outline that view briefly: identify points you strongly disagree with.

- Plan your answer; use one paragraph for each key point.

- **Support the key point** by making reference to/quoting from the passage.

- You can broaden the discussion by using your own knowledge of related events or examples outside the passage. These may provide strong support for your viewpoints.

**Question A**

(iii) Do you think that the age of the writer has an influence on the way he or she expresses his or her opinion? Give reasons. Refer to two of the responses in your answer. (20)

## ◉ Student's Answer Plan

**Tick the points that you will develop in your answer.**

- Rebecca's response – 13 year old.
- Simple, short sentences: 'It's being allowed to do what I want when I want'.
- Language very concrete: 'shoulder', 'room', 'mobile phone'.
- Uses personal pronoun 'I' – freedom means her freedom!
- Jason's response – 20 year old.
- Colourful language, sound effects: 'soothing sound of water against the boat'.
- Idea of inner freedom: 'a state of mind'.
- Language is almost dream-like.
- Links his views with those of Yeats in 'Innisfree'.

**Your own points**

- _____
- _____
- _____

## ◉ Practise Your Answering Skills

**Sample Answer to Question A (iii)**

Write your own answer to this question here.

## 4. THE LANGUAGE OF ARGUMENT

**Study Card No.4:** The Language of Argument

**The Features**

● An argument usually begins with a **statement**. In the statement, the writer may agree or disagree with a particular topic or viewpoint.

● Arguments are supported by **information** that appeal to our **sense of reason**.

● If the information is factual, it will help the writer to prove that the statement is sound or true.

● Many types of evidence may be used in proving that the opening statement is true. **Facts are important in an argument.** We usually know when someone is bluffing. The same goes for writers. If they want their argument to be convincing, they should get their facts right!

● Facts may come from statistics, anecdotes, reports, quotations, etc.

● To show an argument is logical, a step-by-step layout is best. That's why paragraphs are so important.

● **Connective words** such as 'therefore', 'however', 'in addition', and 'on the other hand' are effective at linking one paragraph and idea to another.

● The final part of an argumentative text is the **logical conclusion**.

● If you read a passage with strong reasons to support the opening statement, you may agree with the writer's viewpoint.

● However, you might decide to disagree with a writer's argument. If you do, you need your own reasons to explain why you found the writer's argument unconvincing. For example, the information was unreliable, out of date, inaccurate or incomplete.

● Remember that an opinion is not a fact. That an apple is a fruit is a fact, but that apples are delicious is an opinion. An opinion is a belief or viewpoint. You must learn to distinguish between 'facts' and 'opinions' in your comprehending texts.

## From the Exam Papers

Read and analyse the argumentative passage indicated below (source: Leaving Certificate, Ordinary Level, Sample Paper). Identify examples of some of the features on your Study Card No. 4. Try to say why a particular feature is being used or what it adds to the passage. Finally, read the exam questions on the passage carefully. Underline or highlight the key terms. Make a plan and then answer the three questions. Compare your answers with the sample answers.

The foreword tells you that the text is an extract from a debate. Expect the language of argument and persuasion to feature. The topic is: 'Friendship is still alive in the modern world'. The visual suggests a **formal discussion** is occurring, rather than a conversation among friends on the issue.

Note the **formal introduction**. Speaker A begins by making a statement: 'the idea of friendship is still with us' (agrees with/for the motion).

The speaker defines the word 'friend'.

**Rhetorical question** – note how the phrase 'seriously suggest' shows that the speaker thinks the answer to the question has to be 'No!' Find other examples of rhetorical questioning in the speech.

### SECTION I
### COMPREHENDING (100 marks)

### TEXT 1
### FRIENDSHIP — FOR and AGAINST

Below are extracts from a debate on the motion: "Friendship is still alive in the modern world" Speaker A is arguing for the motion, Speaker B is arguing against the motion.

**Speaker A – For the Motion**

1. Chairman, fellow speakers and friends, I am honoured to be here this evening to speak in this debate. I hope to convince you that the idea of friendship is still with us and that young people, in particular, can still form true and lasting friendships.

2. Before I proceed, however, I would like to tell you what I mean by a friend. Friends have a strong bond of loyalty. You can trust a friend. A friend has time for you. Above all, a friend tells you honestly what she thinks.

3. Do the opposition seriously suggest that these qualities have died in our world? Maybe they haven't looked closely enough. Have they seen the network of friendships that are part of every community whether it's at school, in a sports team or at the office? In these groups it is the little nameless acts of kindness and love that keep the group happy and fulfilled. Indeed, you might say that it is quiet acts of friendship that give the group its true purpose. But there is a bigger sort of friendship. That is the friendship between nations and communities. This type of friendship is growing every year. Thanks to TV and the internet we are aware of people from every part of the globe. Who could see the terrible images from Mozambique and not be moved to offer the hand of friendship?

4. Indeed, in the past decade the Irish have proved themselves to be a friend in deed. Friendship is alive and well! Far from being a thing of the past, it is our only hope for the future.

The speaker gives reasons to prove the statement that friendship is still with us.

The speaker refers to real examples to help prove the point. Are the examples convincing enough? Might they need a bit more detail/explanation to be persuasive?

Very dramatic image, but is it exaggerated? Does such 'evidence' make the point more or less convincing?

Are these facts or opinions?

(i) Refer only to **paragraph** 2 of **Speaker A** as instructed in the question. The question does not ask you simply to summarise her views but to give your opinion of her view. Make two points.

(ii) Outline the different views of the speakers on the internet. Two points would be sufficient here.

(iii) Explain (give reasons) **why** you found one speech more persuasive. For example, you may refer to the facts used to support the opening statement; to the language or techniques used by the speakers, to what connected with your own viewpoint on the issue.

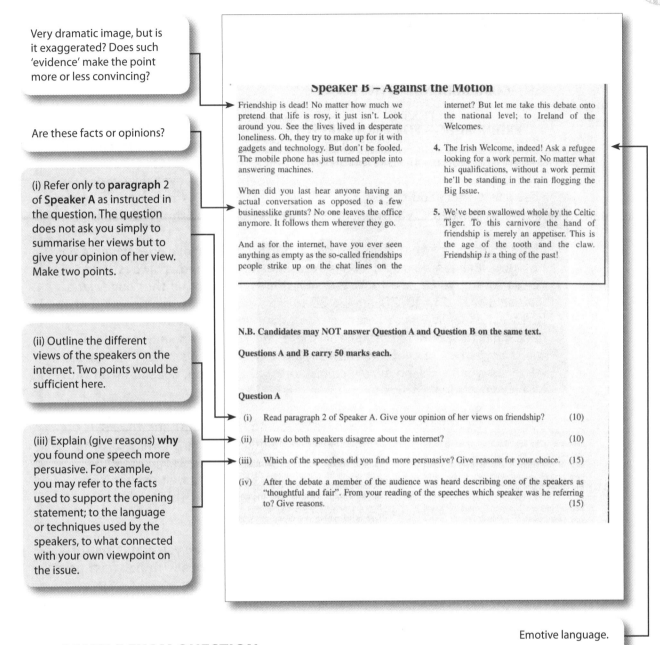

### Speaker B – Against the Motion

Friendship is dead! No matter how much we pretend that life is rosy, it just isn't. Look around you. See the lives lived in desperate loneliness. Oh, they try to make up for it with gadgets and technology. But don't be fooled. The mobile phone has just turned people into answering machines.

When did you last hear anyone having an actual conversation as opposed to a few businesslike grunts? No one leaves the office anymore. It follows them wherever they go.

And as for the internet, have you ever seen anything as empty as the so-called friendships people strike up on the chat lines on the internet? But let me take this debate onto the national level; to Ireland of the Welcomes.

4. The Irish Welcome, indeed! Ask a refugee looking for a work permit. No matter what his qualifications, without a work permit he'll be standing in the rain flogging the Big Issue.

5. We've been swallowed whole by the Celtic Tiger. To this carnivore the hand of friendship is merely an appetiser. This is the age of the tooth and the claw. Friendship *is* a thing of the past!

**N.B. Candidates may NOT answer Question A and Question B on the same text.**

**Questions A and B carry 50 marks each.**

### Question A

(i) Read paragraph 2 of Speaker A. Give your opinion of her views on friendship? (10)

(ii) How do both speakers disagree about the internet? (10)

(iii) Which of the speeches did you find more persuasive? Give reasons for your choice. (15)

(iv) After the debate a member of the audience was heard describing one of the speakers as "thoughtful and fair". From your reading of the speeches which speaker was he referring to? Give reasons. (15)

Emotive language.

## SAMPLE EXAM QUESTION

### Question A

(i) Read paragraph 2 of Speaker A. Give your opinion of her views on friendship. (10)

## ◉ Student's Answer Plan

● Speaker A, paragraph 2 – three points made on what it means to be a friend.

● Loyalty and trust – agree, it's the foundation stone.

● A friend 'has time for you' – disagree – many demands on our friends.

● A friend 'tells you' the truth – not necessarily, a friend knows when to tell the truth.

## ◖◗ Sample Answer to Question A (i)

In paragraph 2, Speaker A makes a number of points on what it means to be a friend in proposing the motion that 'Friendship is still alive in the modern world'.

I strongly agree with the speaker's opening sentence, where she says that 'friends have a strong bond of loyalty'. In my opinion, the loyalty and 'trust' that builds up over time is what cements the friendship between two people. You can have your laughs and your fun and even your moaning sessions with a good friend, but in the end, I think it is the bond of loyalty and trust between you that is central in a strong, healthy friendship.

Her second point, that 'A friend has time for you' is more questionable, in my view. Perhaps we would all like to think that a friend is always there for us. What we choose to forget sometimes, however, is that our friend may be a friend to 10, 20, maybe 30 other people. They don't exist just to be by our side! We must consider the other demands on their time. They need time for work, for study, for sport and for meeting new people. I would not agree, therefore, that a friend should always have time for us. At times when a friend simply cannot be there for you, doesn't mean that he or she suddenly stops being your friend!

Speaker A's third point, a friend 'tells you honestly what she thinks' is an interesting one. Sometimes we want to hear the truth, while at other times, the truth is exactly what we don't want to hear from a friend! Therefore, I think a friend is someone who knows you well enough to be able to judge when to tell the truth, or whether on this particular occasion, a few white lies might be called for.

Speaker A suggests that a friend is loyal, has time for you and is truthful. I would question two of her views, but I strongly agree with her first point on the importance of loyalty and trust in a friendship.

## Answering Techniques

● Begin with a **brief introduction**, setting the context of the question.

● Take each point made by Speaker A and explain why you agree/disagree with it.
  **Note:** you do not have to agree/disagree with every point made by the speaker.

● Use paragraphs.

● Structure each paragraph as follows:
  (a) Identify the point by Speaker A.
  (b) Give your opinion on that point (as instructed by the question).
  (c) Explain why you think this way.

- Take **relevant quotations** from the passage without overdoing it.

- Use your **own words** to develop each paragraph.

- Write **clearly**. Spelling, punctuation, grammar and paragraphing are all awarded marks.

## Question A

(ii)  How do both speakers disagree about the Internet? (10)

## ◉ Student's Answer Plan

**Speaker A**
- Grateful for Internet: 'Thanks to Internet'.
- 'Aware of people from every part of the globe'.
- Led to hand of friendship.

**Speaker B**
- Friendships on chat lines: 'empty'.

## ◉ Sample Answer to Question A (ii)

In the debate, Speaker A and Speaker B make some interesting points about the internet. These points show the internet in a very different light.

Speaker A thinks that we should be thankful for the internet. It has, she argues, made us 'aware of people from every part of the globe'. She supports her point with evidence from Mozambique where images of suffering urged people around the world to offer help, to 'offer', as she puts it, 'the hand of friendship'. The internet, therefore, has helped a 'bigger sort of friendship' to develop and grow – the friendship between nations and communities. This is a very positive view of the internet and its power to bring communities together.

Speaker B, on the other hand, has quite a different viewpoint. I imagine that her opening phrase, 'And as for the internet' is spoken in a very negative and dismissive tone. Her argument is that the internet has encouraged thousands of 'empty', 'so-called friendships' created online. The speaker shows her contempt for chat lines that lead people to make superficial contact with others from around the world, instantly!

Speaker B's view proposes that the internet has done nothing for friendship. This is in complete contrast to Speaker A's more positive view that the internet has enabled people to offer the 'hand of friendship' to people on the other side of the world.

## Answering Techniques

- Begin by rephrasing the question as a statement. This is a useful technique to keep your points focused and relevant to the question.

- Deal with one speaker at a time. Identify the key point made by Speaker A.

- Support the key point by referring to the passage.

- Take relevant quotations from the passage without overdoing it.

- Explain what the reference tells you.

- Now turn to Speaker B's points.

- Once again, refer to or quote from the passage to outline her point on the Internet.

- In your own words, discuss what she is saying.

- Remember to **compare the two views** on the Internet.

### Question A
(iii) Which of the speeches did you find more persuasive? Give reasons for your choice. (15)

## ◉ Student's Answer Plan

**Tick the points that you will develop in your answer.**

- Speaker A more persuasive ☐
- Defines friendship at the beginning ☐
- Facts are well chosen ☐
- Use of rhetorical questions effective ☐
- Balanced, reasonable view ☐
- Uses examples from Ireland and beyond ☐
- Speaker B less persuasive ☐
- Over emotional ☐
- Lacks factual information – mostly personal opinions ☐
- Some viewpoints are too generalised, too extreme – weakens the argument ☐

**Your own points**

- _____
- _____
- _____

## ⦿ Practise Your Answering Skills

### Sample Answer to Question A (iii)

Write your own answer to this question here.

## Question A

(iv) After the debate a member of the audience was heard describing one of the speakers as 'thoughtful and fair'. From your reading of the speeches, which speaker was he referring to? Give reasons. (15)

## ◉ Student's Answer Plan

**Tick the points that you will develop in your answer.**
**Speaker A:**

- Thoughtful. ☐
- Doesn't become too emotional, remains composed. ☐
- Wide range of points – what is a personal friend, opens out to global friendship. ☐
- Good use of examples to support points – Mozambique, Ireland. ☐
- End is very strong with reference to the future. ☐
- Fair. ☐
- Logical, step-by-step approach; well paragraphed. ☐
- Is not dismissive. ☐
- Points are made in a calm way – no need to be too dramatic. ☐

**Your own points**

- _____
- _____
- _____

## ◉ Practise Your Answering Skills

**Sample Answer to Question A (iv)**

Write your own answer to this question here.

_____

_____

_____

_____

_____

## 5. AESTHETIC LANGUAGE

In your exam, an extract from a short story or perhaps a novel may appear as one of the three texts on the exam paper.

### Study Card No.5: Aesthetic Language

### The Features

- Aesthetic texts include stories, poems, song lyrics, plays and novels.
- **Characters** in aesthetic texts can be very interesting. The narrator can tell us about them, while their own dialogue with other characters also reveals aspects of their personalities.
- The setting in a short story or novel is the time and place in which the events occur. Often the setting can have a big influence on the behaviour of the characters in the text.
- Aesthetic language can be very descriptive and creative. Good writers can paint a word picture in a fresh, original and imaginative way.
- Imagery and clear descriptions help to create an atmosphere in the text, e.g. it could be a tense atmosphere, a fearful atmosphere, or a happy atmosphere.
- Adjectives, nouns, verbs and adverbs are carefully selected in describing people, places and action. Look at this example by the writer Khaled Hosseini: 'Just before sunrise, Baba's car peeled into the driveway. His door slammed shut and his running footsteps pounded the stairs'. (*The Kite Runner*)
- Imagery, including metaphors and similes, appear in aesthetic texts. They help to paint vivid word pictures.

## From the Exam Papers

Read and analyse the aesthetic passage below (source: Leaving Certificate, Ordinary Level, Paper 1, 2004.). Identify examples of some of the features on your Study Card No. 5. Try to say why a particular feature is being used or what it adds to the passage. Finally, read the exam questions on the passage, carefully. Underline or highlight the key terms. Make a plan and then answer the three questions. Compare your answers with the sample answers.

The foreword tells you that the text is taken from a **short story** (an extract). It also names the main **characters**, the story's **setting** in addition to outlining the main difficulty facing the characters.

Repetition of the adjective 'grey' matches the mood of the character.

This story is a **third-person narrative**.

Effective **descriptive detail**; note the adjectives, 'shabby' (par.1) 'worn' (par.3) and 'old' (par.4) which suggest Della's poverty.

**Dialogue** is very common in fiction. It brings the characters to life and tells us more about their relationships, their actions, and their motivations.

---

### SECTION I
### COMPREHENDING (100 marks)

#### TEXT I

#### "If only she had more money…"

O. Henry's short story, *The Gift of the Magi*, is set in New York about 100 years ago. Jim and Della are a young married couple. They live in a cheap, rented apartment, and are very short of money, as Jim has taken a big drop in pay. Here is the first part of the story, in edited form.

1. One dollar and eighty-seven cents. That was all. And sixty cents of it was in pennies. Pennies saved one and two at a time by bulldozing the grocer and the vegetable man and the butcher until her cheeks burned. Three times Della counted it. One dollar and eighty-seven cents. And the next day would be Christmas. There was clearly nothing to do but flop down on the shabby little couch and howl. So Della did it.

2. Della finished her cry and powdered her face to hide the blotches. She stood by the window and looked out dully at a grey cat walking a grey fence in a grey backyard. Tomorrow would be Christmas Day, and she had only $1.87 to buy Jim a present. She had been saving every penny she could for months, with this result. Twenty dollars a week doesn't go far. Expenses had been greater than she had calculated. They always are. Only $1.87 to buy a present for Jim. Her Jim. She had spent many a happy hour planning for something nice for him. Something fine and rare. Something just a little bit near to being worthy of the honour of being owned by Jim. If only she had more money. If only…

3. Suddenly she whirled from the window and stood before the mirror. Her eyes were shining brilliantly, but her face had lost its colour within twenty seconds. Rapidly she pulled down her hair and let it fall to its full length. She stood for a long moment in front of the mirror, looking at her beautiful hair, and she thought of how Jim loved to see it like this, rippling and shining like a cascade of brown water. And then she tied it up again nervously and quickly. Once, she hesitated for a minute and stood still while a tear or two splashed on the worn red carpet.

4. Then on went her old brown jacket; on went her old brown hat. With a whirl of skirts and with the brilliant sparkle still in her eyes, she fluttered out the door and down the stairs to the street. She knew exactly what she was looking for. She stopped at the sign that said:
**Madame Sofronie. Hair Goods of All Kinds.**
One flight up Della ran, and waited to catch her breath, so she could say the words clearly.
'Will you buy my hair?' asked Della.
'I buy hair,' said Madame. 'Take yer hat off and let's have a sight of the looks of it.'

Page 2 of 12

**Imagery** – use of simile to paint a graphic picture of Della's hair.

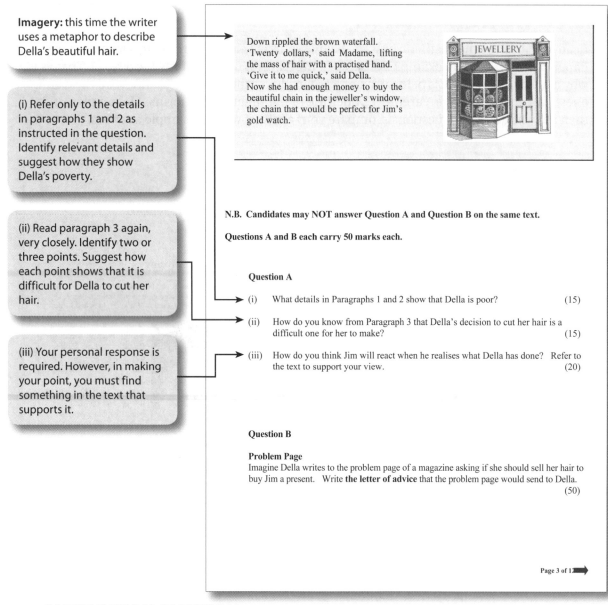

**Imagery:** this time the writer uses a metaphor to describe Della's beautiful hair.

Down rippled the brown waterfall.
'Twenty dollars,' said Madame, lifting the mass of hair with a practised hand.
'Give it to me quick,' said Della.
Now she had enough money to buy the beautiful chain in the jeweller's window, the chain that would be perfect for Jim's gold watch.

JEWELLERY

**(i)** Refer only to the details in paragraphs 1 and 2 as instructed in the question. Identify relevant details and suggest how they show Della's poverty.

N.B. Candidates may NOT answer Question A and Question B on the same text.

Questions A and B each carry 50 marks each.

**Question A**

(i) What details in Paragraphs 1 and 2 show that Della is poor? (15)

**(ii)** Read paragraph 3 again, very closely. Identify two or three points. Suggest how each point shows that it is difficult for Della to cut her hair.

(ii) How do you know from Paragraph 3 that Della's decision to cut her hair is a difficult one for her to make? (15)

**(iii)** Your personal response is required. However, in making your point, you must find something in the text that supports it.

(iii) How do you think Jim will react when he realises what Della has done? Refer to the text to support your view. (20)

**Question B**

**Problem Page**
Imagine Della writes to the problem page of a magazine asking if she should sell her hair to buy Jim a present. Write **the letter of advice** that the problem page would send to Della. (50)

Page 3 of 12

## SAMPLE EXAM QUESTION

### Question A

(i) What details in paragraphs 1 and 2 show that Della is poor?

### ◉ Student's Answer Plan

● Little money, $1.87; had to 'bulldoze' shopkeepers to save a few pennies.

● Counts the money three times in disbelief. She suffered humiliation just to save a few pennies.

● 'Shabby little couch'.

● Bills take most of $20 each week.

**Sample Answer to Question A (i)**

There are several details in paragraphs 1 and 2 that show that Della is poor.

The first suggestion we get that Della is a poor person occurs when the narrator describes Della counting her savings. The phrase 'One dollar and eighty-seven cents' is repeated as if Della just cannot believe how poor her circumstances have become. This is emphasised when we are told that Della counted her savings 'three times'. Not only is this a very meagre amount of money, but sixty cents of it was made up of pennies 'saved one and two at a time'. This shows that Della, being aware of her poverty, had to haggle with shopkeepers in a desperate effort to save some money.

Secondly, I get the impression that Della was humiliated by her constant haggling in order to save the occasional penny. The text tells us she bulldozed and haggled with the butcher and vegetable man 'until her cheeks burned'. It shows the experience was not a positive one for Della. She didn't walk away with a smile on her face knowing she had saved a few pennies. Her poor circumstances forced her to endure this humiliation – and on a regular basis, as 'sixty cents' of it were saved 'one and two at a time'.

It is also a sign of her poverty that she collapsed in tears onto 'a shabby little couch'. Her situation is grim – despite saving 'for months' she had little spare money to buy even a Christmas present. The text refers to the bills mounting up so that 'Twenty dollars a week doesn't go far'. This too shows us that Della has barely enough to buy the essentials while any additional expense reminds her of her poverty and throws her into despair. These details in paragraphs 1 and 2 show clearly, therefore, that Della is poor.

**Answering Techniques**

● Make your opening statement. Rephrase the question as a statement.

● Focus on paragraphs 1 and 2 only as instructed by the question.

● Note that you need to explain your point. **One line is not enough.** Make your point, refer to the text for support then explain in detail.

● As a rough guide, you should write around 15 lines for a 15-mark question (about 100 words).

● Use paragraphs. This makes it easier for the examiner to follow your points.

● Note the phrases used to make the answer more coherent: 'The first suggestion', 'Secondly', 'It is also a sign of'.

- Take relevant quotations from the passage and use them. What do they show about Della's poverty?

- Write clearly. Spelling, punctuation, grammar and paragraphing are all awarded marks.

**Question A**

(ii) How do you know from paragraph 3 that Della's decision to cut her hair is a difficult one for her to make? (15)

## ◎ Student's Answer Plan

- Focus on paragraph 3.

- 'Her face had lost its colour'.

- 'Thought of how Jim loved to see it like this'.

- 'Stood for a long moment admiring her hair' – last look.

- 'Hesitated for a minute . . . tears'.

## ◎ Sample Answer to Question A (ii)

Paragraph 3 of the text shows me in a number of ways that Della's decision to cut her hair is a difficult one.

In the opening of paragraph 3, the narrator tells us that Della's 'face had lost its colour within twenty seconds' of the idea springing into her mind. This tells me that even the thought of cutting her hair, and perhaps her realisation that that was all she could do, was deeply upsetting to her. The prospect of selling her hair was so desperate it drained the blood from her face.

Another indication that Della's decision is a difficult one is shown when she let down her beautiful hair and stood at a mirror, admiring it 'for a long moment'. This suggests to me that she is taking one, long, last, lingering look at her flowing hair that she is shortly about to lose. It shows that her hair means so much to her and even more perhaps to Jim, her husband. What makes Della's decision even more difficult is that Jim, whom she adores, 'loved to see it like this, rippling and shining like a cascade of brown water'.

Finally, at the end of paragraph 3, the narrator describes how Della shed a tear or two as she 'hesitated for a minute and stood still'. This brief moment of indecision, before dressing to go to Madame Sofronie, shows how painful and difficult it would be for Della to cut her hair.

**Answering Techniques**

● Rephrase the question as a statement.

● Focus on paragraph 3 as instructed by the question.

● Making a simple plan before answering will help you to **organise your ideas**.

● Find one piece of evidence to show Della's difficulty. Refer to it/quote it, and then explain how this reference tells you it was a difficult decision.

● When quoting from the passage, only take relevant words/phrases that help to support your point. Do not quote long sentences or passages of three or four lines.

● **Use your own words to develop each paragraph.** Remember to interpret or analyse what you have read in the passage.

● Write clearly. Use short sentences.

## Question A

(iii) How do you think Jim will react when he realises what Della has done? Refer to the text to support your answer. (20)

## ◎ Student's Answer Plan

**Tick the points that you will develop in your answer.**
**Speaker A:**

- Shock and anger – took away what he loved to look at 'Jim loved to see it like this'.  ☐

- Sadness that poverty drove Della to make such a difficult decision.  ☐

- Humbled that she sacrificed for his benefit: 'the chain that would be perfect for Jim's gold watch'.  ☐

- Regret – the chain is no substitute for her flowing hair.  ☐

**Your own points**

- _____
- _____
- _____
- _____
- _____

53

## ◎ Practise Your Answering Skills

### Sample Answer to Question A (iii)

Write your own answer to this question here.

# The Visual Text

**Study Card No.6:** The Visual Text

## The Features

Note that a visual text might include a photograph, cartoon, graphic, chart or painting. The visual element might stand alone or be attached to a written text.

● In preparing to answer on a visual text consider three approaches:

(i) Describe what you see.

(ii) Interpret what you see – here you imagine the story behind the images.

(iii) Think about how and why the images were created.

**1. To describe what you see –** practise the following tasks:
Describe the setting (time and place): day or night, rural or urban, wealthy or poor, etc.
Describe the people and their facial expression: young or old, happy or sad.
Describe the clothes that they wear and the actions that they are performing.
Think about how they react to each other or to the camera. Who are they looking at? At one another, at the viewer, or are they looking into space?
Describe where they are positioned in the photograph. Are they in the foreground or background, to one side or centred?
Describe the situation or action. What can you see happening in the image?

**2. The how and the why**
Was this photograph set up with models who posed for the photographer?
Did the photographer catch a real moment in time?
Why this particular moment? Are the images informative? Or are they trying to 'sell' something: an idea or a product, perhaps?
What do you notice about the angle of the shot? Why might this angle have been chosen?
Why did the photographer use a close-up shot, or a mid-shot or long shot?
Is artificial lighting used? Why?
Comment on the use of colour. Why are certain colours used?
How does colour affect the atmosphere?

**3. Interpreting what you see** – develop your answering skills by practising the following tasks:

- The people:

    Who are the people in the image?

    Why are these particular people (age, looks, attitude, background) captured in the image?

    What do the facial expressions or gestures of the characters tell us?

    Why are the people dressed as they are?

    Why might the people be appealing to young people, to older people, or both?

    Are the people well known or perhaps they may even have celebrity status?

    What are the people thinking right now? Why?

    From what culture or background might the people come?

- The setting:

    What is important about the setting?

    Why are certain properties used in the image?

    Is the setting a desirable place or not?

- The situation:

    How might the situation in the image have arisen?

    What story is 'told' by the images? What view of life is suggested or represented by the images?

    What might occur after the photograph was taken?

    What impression (positive or negative) of life is suggested by the images?

    Do the images show a specific theme or idea?

    Are they well-chosen images to represent this theme?

- Opinion – personal response:

    Could you add another image that would show the theme effectively?

    What effect did the images have on your thoughts and feelings?

    Would you have a favourite/least favourite image?

> **Remember: Images may be accompanied by a short written text, or include captions. A caption is like a headline that accompanies the image. Captions will connect with the theme of the Text.**

 **Exam Trends**

 ## Most Frequently Asked Exam Questions on the Visual Text

**Note:** In more recent years, a visual element has appeared to illustrate a written text more often than as a stand-alone text by itself.

### Write a description of an image

- By referring to the visual details in the cartoon, explain what you think has happened in Image 1, on page four. Support your answer with evidence from the cartoon. (2013)

- 'Write a clear and detailed description of any one of the four images in Text 3.' (2010)

- 'Choose one of the six images in Text 3 and clearly describe what you see.' (2007)

- 'Choose one of the other images from the text and write a clear description of it.' (2005)

- 'Write a clear description of any one of the four images.' (2004)

- 'Choose the image that you think is the one that most young people would recognise. Describe that image.' (2003)

- 'Choose another pair of images and clearly describe each image in it.' (2002)

### Explain if an image is or is not a good representation of the theme of Text 3

- 'Choose one of the images from Text 3 and explain why you think it is or is not a good illustration of that type of connection.' (2009)

- 'Which image best captures the idea of success for you? Explain your answer.' (2007)

- 'Select the image from Text 3 that best expresses the idea of freedom for you. Give a reason for your choice.' (2005)

- 'Hoping for Money. Which of the four images do you think shows this most strongly? Give reasons for your choice.' (2004)

- 'Which pair of images do you think is best at expressing the idea of change? Explain your choice.' (2002)

- 'Choose an image that best captures your sense of the future. Explain your choice.' (2001)

### Write a personal response to the images, e.g. best, worst, effective, favourite image, etc.

- The cartoon featuring Fifi the dog (Image 2, on page five) prompted some critical letters when it was published. Do you find this cartoon funny or disturbing or both? Explain your answer with reference to the cartoon. (2013)

- Look at the Google logo at the top of this text. Do you think it is an effective or appealing logo? Support your answer with reference to the logo. (2012)

- 'Which one of the different types of connection represented in Text 3 do you find most interesting? Explain your answer.' (2009)

- 'If you were one of the judges of the competition, which of these photographs would you select as an overall winner? Explain your decision.' (2008)

- 'Write a response to the collection of images using one of the following prompts:
  - They are funny because . . .
  - They are scary because . . .
  - They are exciting because . . .' (2006)

- 'Which type of entertainment pictured above most appeals to you? Explain your choice.' (2003)

## Replacing or adding an image

- Describe an image (photo, painting, drawing, etc.) that could be used to illustrate this extract, which would capture the atmosphere you described in (a) above. (2011)

- Describe an image (photo, painting, drawing, etc.) that could be used to illustrate this extract, which would capture the atmosphere you described in (a) above. (2011)

- 'If you were asked to replace one of the images illustrating a connection in Text 3, which one would you choose to remove? Describe the image you would use as a replacement.' (NB The caption should remain the same.) (2009)

- 'You have been asked to add another image of success to this collection. What image would you choose? Give reasons for your answer.' (2007)

- 'Imagine you were asked to add another image of freedom to the collection. What image would you suggest? Explain why you would choose that image.' (2005)

## Other questions of interpretation

- What does Image 1 show us about Brian O'Driscoll as a sportsman? Explain your answer with reference to the image. (2012)

- From what you see in the images that illustrate this text, identify a skill or quality that you think a president would need to carry out his or her official duties. Explain your answer. (2012)

- 'Which of the situations pictured in Text 3 would you least like to find yourself in? Explain your answer.' (2010)

- 'Do these photographs convey a positive or negative impression overall of modern Irish lifestyle? Give reasons for your answer.' (2008)

- 'Look at the images. In your opinion, do they represent an exciting or a frightening view of the future? Give reasons for your answer.' (2001)

## Write a caption to accompany the images

- 'Write a caption to accompany any three of the four images that appear in Text 3. You should label each caption with the number (1, 2, 3 or 4) that appears on the corresponding image.' (2010)

## Questions that link the visual and written text

- 'Do you think that the visual text helps to support the writer's view? Give a reason.' (2006)

## Imagine you are one of the people in the text

- 'Look at the image of The Beggar and the Businessman. Imagine that you are either the beggar or the businessman. Write down what your thoughts are at this moment.' (2004)

## From the Exam Papers

Read and interpret the visual text below (source: Visual Texts in the Leaving Certificate Ordinary Level, Paper 1, 2010). As you practise answering these and other visual text questions, tick off the skills and tasks described in Study Card No. 6. Make sure you also write a few sample answers on the visual text questions above from past exam papers. As usual, underline or highlight the key terms. Make a brief plan before answering the question. Compare your answers with the sample answers.

The theme of the text is facing danger. Each of the images will link with this theme in some way.

Note that each image has a number. Refer to the number to quickly and clearly identify which image you want to discuss.

Remember the skills you practised from your Study Card No. 6. Use the answering skills that you developed from practising answers before the exam.

Read the questions on the images very carefully. They will help you to study the images in a more focused way.

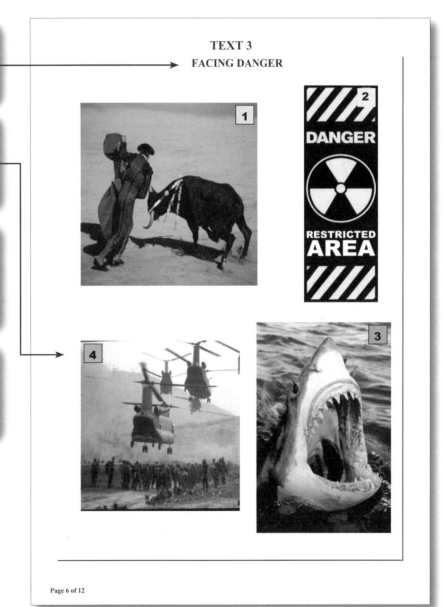

**TEXT 3**
**FACING DANGER**

Page 6 of 12

(i) Describe only **one** of the images; a clear and detailed description is required. Focus on the content and the composition of the image. Write about 15 lines.

(ii) **Three** captions are required. Remember to label each caption as instructed. Note that the photo numbers go in a clockwise direction.

(iii) Choose a situation in **one** image. Describe what is happening and explain why you would not like to be there.

---

**N.B. Candidates may NOT answer Question A and Question B on the same text.**

**Questions A and B carry 50 marks each.**

**Question A**

(i)   Write a clear and detailed description of any **one** of the four images in Text 3.                                                              (15)

(ii)  Write a caption to accompany any **three** of the four images that appear in Text 3.
You should label each caption with the number (1, 2, 3 or 4) that appears on the corresponding image.                                      (15)

(iii) Which of the situations pictured in Text 3 would you least like to find yourself in?
Explain your answer.                                                          (20)

**Question B**

**Holiday of a lifetime**

You work for a company that specialises in activity holidays like bungee-jumping, rock-climbing, going on safari, etc.  Write a piece to appear on a webpage promoting an exciting adventure holiday anywhere in the world.                (50)

## SAMPLE EXAM QUESTION

### Question A

(i)   Write a clear and detailed description of any one of the four images in Text 3. (15)

## ◉ Student's Answer Plan

- Chosen image – number 4 – military subject.
- The content – people, setting, helicopter.
- Foreground – military helicopters.
- Centre – soldiers – backpacks, army gear, weapons.
- Background – wooded hills – dust clouds.
- The composition:
    - Long shot.
    - Colours – grey/green.
    - Natural lighting.
    - Gritty quality.

## ◉ ▪ Sample Answer to Question A (i)

The image that I would like to describe is image 4. This image is a long shot of a military subject. It links with the theme of Text 3, Facing Danger.

The first objects I see in this image are five large, military helicopters hovering over an assembly of soldiers. Most of the helicopters seem to be leaving the scene. The large helicopter in the foreground, however, is about to land. The helicopters are coloured grey/green, similar to the khaki colours of the soldiers' uniforms. The helicopters are very close together and they are creating a dust cloud in the centre of the photograph.

I can also see a large group of approximately 50 or more soldiers gathered beneath the helicopters. In this long shot, none of the soldiers can be identified individually as they are not facing the camera. They are standing anonymously on a dusty roadway, on flat land, surrounded by some low, wooded hills in the background. The soldiers are dressed in full army uniform, with some of them wearing short-sleeved tops. They are carrying backpacks and communication kit. Some of the soldiers have aerials projecting from their kit.

Many of the soldiers are wearing hard helmets, the type that offers protection in combat or dangerous situations. However, the soldiers are not panicking at all, and seem quite subdued. They are waiting to be picked up by the helicopters in the foreground.

The main colours in the image are various tones of grey and green. There is no evidence of artificial lighting that I can see. The image was taken in daylight although the sky in the background is overcast. I see that the photographer was at a distance from the scene. The image does seem a little out of focus, so a zoom lens may have been used. The focus of the image is certainly the large helicopters and the gathering of soldiers on the ground. The photograph has a 'gritty', real-life quality to it.

**Answering Techniques**

- Make your opening statement. Rephrase the question as a statement.

- Focus on what you see.

- Note that you can see the 'what' of the image (the content of the image). However, you can also see 'how' the image was created (the composition of the image).

- Begin your description by focusing on the content of the image.

- Next, describe how the image was put together (the composition).

- You may use words such as foreground, centre, or background to locate features of the image.

- Write clearly. Spelling, punctuation, grammar and paragraphing are all awarded marks.

**Question A**

(ii) Write a caption to accompany any three of the four images that appear in Text 3 [on page 59]. You should label each caption with the number (1, 2, 3, or 4) that appears on the corresponding image. (15)

## ◉ Student's Answer Plan

- Image 1 – Old enemies can be deadly dangerous.

- Image 3 – Dangers of the Deep – Stay Back!

- Image 4 – For real.

## Sample Answer to Question A (ii)

> The three images that I wish to write a caption for are images 1, 3 and 4.
>
> My caption for image 1 is: Old enemies can be deadly dangerous. I think this caption would emphasise that while a bullfighter may have years of experience in the ring, he must always approach the bull with great caution on every occasion.
>
> I think a suitable caption for image 3 might be: Dangers of the Deep – Stay Back! This caption might suggest that sharks usually attack humans when we stray into their territory. The gaping jaws of the shark show that we are not welcome.
>
> My final caption is for image 4. I think the caption that would be appropriate is: For real. This caption shows that a real war is no training exercise, so soldiers must be prepared for anything

## Answering Techniques

- While the question does not ask you to explain your captions, you may offer a brief explanation of each if you wish.

## Question A

(iii) Which of the situations pictured in Text 3 would you least like to find yourself in? Explain your answer. (20)

## Student's Answer Plan

**Tick the points that you will develop in your answer.**
**Image 3**

- In deep water, miles from shore. ☐
- Dangerous situation – life threatening/fatal. ☐
- Shark's territory not mine. ☐

**Your own points**

- _____
- _____
- _____

### ⊙ Sample Answer to Question A (iii)

Of the four situations pictured in Text 3, the one I would least like to find myself in is image 3, featuring the shark!

My first reaction to this image is one of terror! The image captures the raw power and sheer menace of what appears to be a killing machine. This situation would not be very appealing to me for a number of reasons.

Firstly, I imagine that the shark is swimming miles offshore in the deep blue sea. Being in deep water, and with only a Level 1 Certificate in Swimming competence from my old primary school, I don't think I would ever out swim this beast if it came to a head to head. Moreover, speaking of heads, I can just imagine mine fitting nicely inside the mouth of my opponent, tucked in behind those impressive, white incisors.

In addition, it would be completely pointless and useless to try calling for help when the nearest boat is one hour away and the shark is ready for dinner – right now! I would also imagine that any encounter with this fearsome shark – look at those triangular teeth – would be fatal, for me, not the shark! The sea is his domain, not mine. I am the one trespassing here and I cannot expect much mercy from a five-ton killer shark.

Some might argue that it would be a rare privilege to get up close to such a powerful and beautiful creature of the wild. I say, that's fine for 'some'. However, I prefer my sharks inside an aquarium, where I can munch my popcorn and make rude faces at the beast on the other side of a six-foot glass wall. Wild beasts such as sharks are hunters. I would prefer to be anywhere else in the world rather than bobbing along in a flimsy boat, floating into their habitat and terrified at the thought of becoming part of nature's food chain.

### Answering Techniques

- Identify the image on which you wish to answer.
- Describe your immediate reaction to the photograph.
- Explain, giving three reasons (20-mark question), why the situation is not appealing to you.
- This student has taken a humorous approach. You could take a more serious approach if you wish.
- Note that the points made, in a humorous way, are quite valid and sound reasons why not to be in the situation.

# Language Categories

## ◐ Main Language Categories in Comprehending, Question A

**Note:** Many comprehending texts include more than one type of language. For example, a story extract may be narrative but also informative. The table below simply shows the main types of language in the comprehending texts.

| | Information | Narration | Persuasion | Argument | Aesthetic | Visual text |
|---|---|---|---|---|---|---|
| Dept. Sample Paper | | | | Text 1 Debate | Text 2 Novel extract | Text 3 *Theme:* Moments of friendship – 4 images |
| 2001 | Text 1 Interview | | Text 2 Opinions on 'computerised hotels' | | | Text 3 *Theme:* Future Times – 6 images plus written element |
| 2002 | Text 2 Newspaper article | | | | Text 1 Novel extract | Text 3 *Theme:* Changes – 10 images |
| 2003 | Text 1 Concert review | | Text 2 Opinions on entertainment | | | Text 3 *Theme:* Entertaining the World – 6 images |
| 2004 | Text 2 Newspaper article | | | | Text 1 Short story extract | Text 3 *Theme:* Hoping for Money – 4 images |
| 2005 | | Text 2 Story extract | Text 1 Opinions on freedom | | | Text 3 *Theme:* Images of Freedom – 6 images |
| 2006 | Text 1 Research results | | | | Text 2 Novel extract | Text 3 *Theme:* The Horror Industry – collage of 5 images plus written element |

| | Information | Narration | Persuasion | Argument | Aesthetic | Visual text |
|---|---|---|---|---|---|---|
| 2007 | **Text 2** Interview | **Text 1** Biography | | | | **Text 3** *Theme*: Faces of Success – 6 images |
| 2008 | | **Text 1** Story extract | **Text 2** Influence of technology | | | **Text 3** *Theme*: Irish Lifestyle – 6 images |
| 2009 | **Text 1** Interview | **Text 2** Memoir | | | | **Text 3** *Theme*: Types of Connection – 6 images |
| 2010 | **Text 1** Description | **Text 2** Real-life adventure | | | | **Text 3** *Theme*: Facing Danger – 4 images |
| 2011 | **Text 2** Diary | **Text 1** Memoir | | **Text 3** Introduction to short stories | | Questions on images under each of the three texts |
| 2012 | **Text 2** Presidential Letter | | **Text 1** Information and opinion on sporting leader | **Text 3** Information and argument on Google | | Questions on images under each of the three texts |
| 2013 | **Text 2** Description | **Text 1** Memoir **Text 3** Autobiography | | | | Questions on images under Text 2 |

# Key Exam Tips

## Key Exam Tips and Techniques for Comprehending, Question A

- Expect to see three texts in Section 1, Comprehending, Question A.

- Carefully select one text on which to answer.

- On your exam paper, write down your time allowance for each question, beside the actual question.

- Read the text, at least twice. After your first reading, read the questions. Then reread the text with more focus.

- Many questions ask you to answer on the:
  - Content of the passage (what is written).
  - Style of the writer (how it is written).
  - Purpose of the passage (why it written)
- You can also expect a question inviting a personal response to the text.
- Read every question on your text very carefully. Note the marks for each question. Questions with more marks expect a little more detail in the answer.
- As a general guideline, write about 15 lines for a 15-mark question. For a 20-mark question, write around 20 lines.
- Underline or highlight the key instructions in the question.
- In your answer, you must focus on following these instructions.
- Plan your answer – most questions expect two or three key points.
- Look at your plan. Make sure it deals with each part of the question. Start to write your full answer only after completing your plan.
- Make each key point in a paragraph of its own.
- To develop your point, refer to/quote from the passage. Then discuss the reference/quote and say what it shows you.
- Always refer to the passage in support of your points.
- When quoting from the passage, use quotation marks to show this.
- Don't quote large chunks of text – select your key words or phrases that will best support your points.
- Remember the key point about PCLM: *what* you write is important, but *how* you write will also earn you marks.
- Write clearly and legibly, and pay attention to accurate spelling and grammar. And of course, *don't forget to use paragraphs!*

## Record of What I Have Learned Revising for Paper 1, Section 1, Comprehending, Question A

### How Writers Use Language

**Main features of language categories are:**
- **Language of information**

  - _____
  - _____
  - _____
  - _____

● **Language of narration**

  ▪ _____

  ▪ _____

  ▪ _____

  ▪ _____

● **Language of persuasion**

  ▪ _____

  ▪ _____

  ▪ _____

  ▪ _____

● **Language of argument**

  ▪ _____

  ▪ _____

  ▪ _____

  ▪ _____

● **Aesthetic use of language**

  ▪ _____

  ▪ _____

  ▪ _____

  ▪ _____

● **Visual texts**

  ▪ _____

  ▪ _____

  ▪ _____

  ▪ _____

## Main things I must remember while answering a question on a passage:

● **Before writing my answer**

  ▪ _____

  ▪ _____

  ▪ _____

  ▪ _____

● **While writing my answer**

  ▪ _____

  ▪ _____

  ▪ _____

  ▪ _____

● **After writing my answer**

  ▪ _____

  ▪ _____

  ▪ _____

  ▪ _____

● **Main things to remember while answering on a visual text**

  ▪ _____

  ▪ _____

  ▪ _____

  ▪ _____

Well done on completing this section! Our next chapter deals with Comprehending, Question B.

**Date completed:**

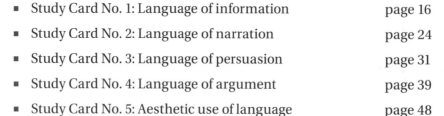

## Around 50 Minutes Revision

Revise your Study Cards. You will find these on the following pages:

## Around 20 Minutes Revision
### (for each worked exam paper)

● It would be a good idea to study again the four key steps to take in improving your comprehending skills.

- **Step 1**
  Reread the way questions were broken down, underlined/highlighted in this section.

- **Step 2**
  Reread the sample answer **plans** in this section.

- **Step 3**
  Reread the **sample answers** in this section.

- **Step 4**
  Reread the **answering techniques** in this section.

## Around 5 Minutes
### (Check your Time Management)

● Suggested timing for each section:

- Section 1, Question A – overall time allowance = 50 minutes (includes reading time and planning time)

- Question (i) – approximate time = 15 minutes

- Question (ii) – approximate time = 15 minutes

- Question (iii) – approximate time = 20 minutes

# Chapter 3

## Paper 1, Sec. I – Comprehending: Question B

This chapter contains the following items. You should tick the boxes as you complete each.

- Introduction ☐
- RPTA: Key Tips to Maximise Your Marks ☐
- Write a Talk or Speech ☐
- Write a Description or Opinion Piece ☐
- Write a Diary or Blog ☐
- Write a Personal Letter ☐
- Write a Formal Letter ☐
- Write a Feature Article ☐
- Write a Newspaper Report ☐
- Write a Review ☐
- Write a Formal Report ☐
- Write an Advertisement ☐
- Key Exam Tips ☐
- Your Last Minute Revision! ☐

# Introduction

Section 1, Comprehending: Question B, is essentially a functional writing task. Browse the table of previous exam questions to see which tasks have been most popular on the paper.

There are great tips on your Study Cards, which are an easy, convenient and efficient way to prepare for different types of writing task in Question B. Revise the tips closely and study the sample answers that show you how it's done. Practise your own answers and compare your answers with those in the text.

This is a 50-mark question and one for which you will be rewarded handsomely if you use appropriate language for your specific audience and meet the purpose of your writing task. In this chapter, you will also see examples of how to use a conventional layout for texts such as magazine articles, newspaper articles, formal letters and so on.

 **At a Glance**

 **What Is Question B?**

Question B is a functional writing task – to write, for example, a short talk or speech, a description, the copy for an advertisement, a diary or blog, a personal or formal letter, a newspaper article, a review or a report.

 **How Many Marks, How Much Time?**

Question B is worth 50 marks.
Suggested time for planning and writing your answer is 35 minutes.

## General Advice

Whichever Question B you answer in the exam, there are a few general points that are worth remembering for any functional writing task. These points will be discussed in more detail later in the chapter.

- Use language with an appropriate register. This means that you must write in a suitable tone and with appropriate vocabulary for the **specific task** and **audience**. Decide, therefore, if your language should be chatty, or relaxed, or more formal before you begin writing.

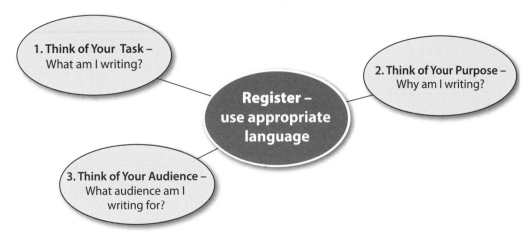

1. **Think of Your Task** – What am I writing?

2. **Think of Your Purpose** – Why am I writing?

3. **Think of Your Audience** – What audience am I writing for?

**Register – use appropriate language**

- Have a clear sense of your **audience**. Read the question carefully. Most questions tell you who your audience is.

- Write with a strong sense of **purpose**. Be clear about why you are writing. Again, the question usually tells you why you are writing.

- Write what you are instructed to write. There is no point (and few marks) for writing a diary if the question asks for a letter.

- **Brainstorm** ideas and make a **plan**.

- Arrange your ideas into paragraphs. Give your writing a shape or **layout** that meets accepted standards (e.g. for a letter, the placing of the address in the top right-hand corner).

- Keep your sentences **clear** and **concise**.

- **Punctuate accurately** and observe the rules of grammar.

- **Keep your answer focused**. Check, while planning, that each paragraph is **relevant** to the question.

- While writing, before you begin each paragraph, refer back to your plan to guide you. This will also help you to keep focused on the question.

- If you have time at the end, take a few minutes to reread your answer and make any minor changes where required.

## Exam Trends

### Recent Trends in Paper 1, Section 1, Question B, English Ordinary Level

| | Dept. Sample Paper | 2001 | 2002 | 2003 | 2004 | 2005 | 2006 | 2007 | 2008 | 2009 | 2010 | 2011 | 2012 | 2013 |
|---|---|---|---|---|---|---|---|---|---|---|---|---|---|---|
| Talk or speech | | | | | ✓ | | ✓ | | ✓ | ✓ | ✓ | ✓ | ✓ | ✓ |
| Description | | ✓ | ✓✓ | ✓ | | | | | ✓ | | ✓ | ✓ | | |
| Advertisement | | | | | | ✓ | | | | | ✓ | | | |
| Diary or blog | ✓ | | ✓ | | ✓ | ✓ | | ✓ | | ✓ | | | ✓ | |
| Personal letter | ✓✓ | | | | ✓ | | | | | ✓ | | | | |
| Formal letter | | ✓ | | ✓ | | | | | ✓ | | | ✓ | ✓ | ✓ |
| Newspaper feature article | | ✓ | | | | | | ✓ | | | | | | |
| News report | ✓ | ✓ | | | | | ✓ | ✓ | | | | | | |
| Review | | | | ✓ | | | ✓ | | | | | | | ✓ |
| Formal Report | | | | | | ✓ | | | | ✓ | | | | |

# RPTA

## Key Tips to Maximise your Marks

> **RPTA:**
> Read
> Plan
> Time
> Answer

> Remember, you may not answer a
> Question A and a Question B on the same text!

## Key Tip 1: READ the Question Correctly

- You only answer one question in Question B, so it is extremely important that you read the question very closely. If you misread the question here, your answer will score very low marks.

- When you read your question, there are THREE essential things to work out – the *what*, the *who* and the *why*!

### 1. WHAT are you instructed to write?

If the question tells you to write a letter, then you must write a letter! Not a speech, nor an essay, nor a diary. This is basic, but in the pressure of an exam, it is surprising how many students do not write what they are asked to write.

**HINT** Make sure you know exactly what the purpose of your writing task is and for what audience you are writing.

### 2. WHO are you writing for?

Many of the questions tell you who your audience is, in other words, who you are writing for. This is important because it helps you to plan both *what* you are going to write and *how* you are going to write it.

For example, if you were asked to write a talk for a group of First Year students on good study habits, then the points you make (what you write) must make sense to 12 and 13 year olds. Also, the language you use (how you write) must be understood by that age group.

### 3. WHY are you writing?

In reading your question, be clear about the purpose of your writing, in other words, why you are writing. Is it to inform, or to entertain, perhaps to persuade or describe something? Most questions tell you this. A knowledge of why you are writing helps to keep your answer focused and relevant.

Be very careful to answer the question asked. Therefore, read your Question B at least three times, then underline or highlight the key terms in that question. Make sure that you know what you are writing, who you are writing for, and why you are writing. Only then, should you begin to work on your answer plan.

## Key Tip 2: PLAN Your Answer

- In planning what to write, make sure your points are relevant and appropriate. Do not include points that would be unsuitable for your audience. Also, do not use examples that would mean little or nothing to your audience or, worse still, that might confuse your audience.

- In planning, be clear about why you are writing – the function or purpose of your writing. Are you writing to complain or to congratulate, to persuade or to inform, to console or to inspire? The points you include in your plan must be appropiate to your purpose.

Irrelevant content will not be awarded high marks!
In your plan, make sure your points will make sense to your audience.

## Key Tip 3: TIME Your Answer

Time Allowed (Paper 1):
2 Hours 50 Minutes

- The suggested time for **Section I Comprehending, Question B** (50 marks) is approximately 35 minutes, this includes planning time.

## Key Tip 4: ANSWER the Question Asked

- Just before you begin to write your full answer, look once again at the question, then at your plan. If you think your plan is not directly answering each key term or instruction in the question, you have time to make slight changes now.

- **CHECKLIST**

  - Make sure you are writing what you were asked to write, for example, a letter, or talk, or newspaper article. ☐

  - Make sure you are aware of your audience.
    Your content and language must be appropriate to this audience. ☐

  - Make sure you know why you are writing. ☐

  - Check again your time allowance for the question, and then begin. ☐

# Write a Talk or Speech

## What Kind of Questions to Expect

Here are some of the questions on talks from past exam papers.

● Write the text of a talk you would give at a happy family event, in which you recall some of your important family memories. (50) (LC, OL, 2013, Question B)

● Imagine you are running for election as leader of the Student Council in your school. Write the talk you would deliver to your school assembly outlining the qualities you feel you possess that would make you an excellent leader of the Student Council. (50) (LC, OL, 2012, Question B)

● Write the talk you would give to a group of students from different countries visiting your school, in which you explain to them what it is like to live in Ireland today. (50) (LC, OL, 2011, Question B)

● **People need to be motivated in order to face a challenge.**
Imagine your class is considering undertaking a 10 kilometre cross-county run for a charity of you choice. Write a short talk to inspire them to take up this challenge. (50) (LC, OL, 2010, Question B)

● Write the short **talk** you would give to your class on **one** of the following topics:

  ▪ Letter writing is a thing of the past.

  ▪ The internet can be a fascinating place.

  ▪ There is nothing in newspapers to interest young people. (50) (LC, OL, 2009, Question B)

● Write the talk you would give to your classmates encouraging them to take up photography as a hobby. (50) (LC, OL, 2008, Question B)

● **A Class Talk**
Imagine you were asked to give a talk to younger students about how they might deal with some common childhood fears. Write the talk that you would give. (50) (LC, OL, 2006, Question B)

● Your community has been offered €100,000 for use on any local project. Write the **speech** that you would make to a meeting of your Local Community Association in which you outline the project that you think the money should be spent on. (50) (LC, OL, 2004, Question B)

## Study Card No.7: How to Write a Successful Talk or Speech

- Having read your question carefully, make sure you are clear about your:
  - **Subject**: *what* you are writing about.
  - **Audience**: *who* you are writing for.
  - **Purpose**: *why* you are writing.

- Plan what you are going to write or say. Do not try to include too many ideas, which may confuse your audience. In your plan, ask yourself, are my points relevant and interesting?

- Include ideas or points that will inform, entertain and/or persuade your audience. If you think any points are weak or irrelevant, delete them from your plan.

- Aim to focus on three or four key areas, each one developed into a paragraph. You will need an introduction, the main body of your talk (two or three paragraphs), and a conclusion.

- Begin by welcoming your audience. Introduce yourself. Say why you are here, what you are going to speak about.

- Think carefully about the best type of language to use. After working out the what, who, and why above, you then have to decide on how you are going to make your points. In a talk, you may use all five language categories. If the talk is informal, you should use more chatty and relaxed language.

- When using **informative language**, remember to write clearly. Use information from a variety of sources.

- When using **persuasive language**, remember to create a particular tone: anger, joy, outrage, disbelief, and so on. Include phrases such as: 'I'm sure you'll agree with me that', 'You are all reasonable people, so', The situation is totally unacceptable'. In an inspirational speech, use repetition to highlight your key point: 'We can do this, we must do this, we will do this.'

- When using **narrative language**, remember to include an anecdote or simple description of your or another person's experience. This can be very memorable and draw the audience into the talk. Personal stories may also be very emotive and win over your audience.

- When using **argumentative language**, remember to include facts to help to prove a point.

- When using **aesthetic language**, remember to include one of two images to paint a clear picture in the listener's mind.

- Near the end of your talk, **briefly summarise your key points**, then remind the audience how they will benefit from your advice. Finally, thank them for their time and attention.

- If writing a speech, you may want to use language that is more formal. In a debate, you can begin your speech with 'Chairperson, adjudicators, members of the opposition/proposition' or 'Ladies and gentlemen'.

## From the Exam Papers

Read **Question B** below from the 2010 paper. Underline or highlight the key terms of the question. Work out *what* you have to write, *who* you are writing for, and *why* you are writing. These three factors will help you to decide *how* to write your talk.

Make a plan and then write your talk. Compare your talk with the sample talk below.

*Who?* You are writing for **your class**.

*What?* Write a **short talk**.

*Why?* You are writing to **inspire/motivate** your class to take up the challenge of a 10-km race.

---

I had to carry my own food and camping equipment. This included large quantities of energy drinks, freeze-dried food, plus a change of running clothes, all packed into a 30 litre rucksack. By the end of the race my arms, legs and stomach were completely shredded.

We faced the danger of heat exhaustion every day. The temperature regularly reached 30°C. For most of us, the second last stage was the worst: 54 miles of tortuous hills, jungle, two water crossings and hot, sandy ground to finish. To top it all off, I picked up a tummy bug from swallowing water when I was wading through a swamp.

I was just running along being sick in the dark. There was no one around. It felt like the stage was never going to end. Twenty-three hours later I reached the finish line.

But I was also a little sad that it was over. I loved the bond with the other runners. At times like that you make friends really quickly. It truly was my toughest challenge and finishing it gave me a great sense of achievement."

**N.B. Candidates may NOT answer Question A and Question B on the same text.**

**Questions A and B carry 50 marks each.**

**Question A**

(i) Based on your reading of the passage, give **three** reasons why you think the Amazon River is described as terrifying and dangerous. Explain your answer with reference to the text. (15)

(ii) Martin Strel and Sophie Collett are both remarkable people. From what you have read about them in the above texts would you agree with this statement? Give reasons for your answer. (15)

(iii) Both Strel and Collett took many risks in the course of their activities. In your opinion, what makes people want to undertake such dangerous activities? Give reasons for your answer. (20)

**Question B.**
People need to be motivated in order to face a challenge.
Imagine your class is considering undertaking a 10 kilometre cross-country run for a charity of your choice. Write a short talk to inspire them to take up this challenge. (50)

Page 3 of 12 ➡

---

## ◎ Student's Answer Plan – Five or Six Short Paragraphs

● Introduction – introduce myself; say why I am here.

● Paragraph 2 – explain that 10 km is a big challenge – difficult.

- Paragraph 3 – show class we can do it – last year's success; determination.
- Paragraph 4 – preparations – train hard and get sponsors.
- Paragraph 5 – who'll benefit: the charity and ourselves too.
- Conclusion – thank everyone; confident of success.

**Note on language:** Use informal, chatty language. Focus on information, narrative and persuasion.

## Sample Answer to Question B

Good morning everyone and thank you Mr Hyland for giving me a few minutes to speak to our class today. I want to talk to you briefly about the 10-km run which we have been considering this week.

One of the questions I have heard over the last few days is, are we trying to do too much? I understand that some of you are anxious about completing a 10-km run. I can see why many students might feel it is a challenge that is bound to fail. It is something we, as a class, have never done before, and the last thing we want to do is let down this year's charity.

I can see where people with doubts are coming from. However, I believe that the 10-km run will be a success exactly because it is such a challenge. I am sure everyone in this class knows how successful last year's marathon basketball match was. You all remember how difficult it was to play continuously for 10 hours. But we succeeded. Together, we took on that challenge, and it certainly was worth it, because we raised over €3,000 for our local Wheelchair Association. OK, the 10 km might be in a different league. But in this class, we do not turn down challenges; we accept them and face them head on.

So, what do we have to do? The first thing we can do is to prepare ourselves for the challenge. Mr Hyland has organised cross-country training every Tuesday and Thursday after school. I think every single one of us should be out there, doing our bit. We have five weeks to prepare, so let's prepare. The second thing is to get as many sponsors as possible. Our target this year is €5,000 for the St Vincent de Paul society. It is an ambitious target, but we can achieve it, we must achieve it, and I'm confident that we will achieve it!

Finally, can I remind you that we too benefit from this challenge? I know we are a determined class, a strong class and a united class. After the 10-km run, we should be a much fitter class! I know we can do this, and I know we will do this. If we pull together, the 10-km challenge will be a tough but fantastic event and something that we can be very proud of organising.

Classmates, thank you for your attention. I look forward to your support and participation in the exciting challenge that awaits us.

## Answering Techniques

- **Greet the target audience** in an appropriate way. Introduce yourself and explain why you are here.

- Address the concerns of the audience.

- **Use language that creates a relaxed atmosphere** – audience is the speaker's own peers.

- Remind the class of previous successes.

- **Inspire** the audience – make them believe they can do it.

- List the preparations necessary to make it a success.

- Finish with benefits for class and thank audience for attention. Note use of repetition.

- A reminder! Spelling, punctuation, grammar and paragraphing are awarded marks too.

# Write a Description or Opinion Piece

## What Kind of Questions to Expect

Here are some of the questions on descriptions from past exam papers:

- Imagine that you have been selected as a space-ship crew member. There is limited living space aboard the space-ship. Therefore, you must carefully choose the things you would take on your voyage into space. Write a list of up to five things you would choose to take with you. Explain and justify your choices. (50) (LC, OL, 2011, Question B)

- A competition has been announced to select crew members for a new *Brendan* voyage. In approximately 250 words, explain to Tim Severin why you should be chosen as a crew member for this voyage. (50) (LC, OL, 2010, Question B)

- Write about the invention from the past which you think has had the greatest influence on our present-day lifestyle. (50) (LC, OL, 2008, Question B)

- Write the answer you would give to the question: what does entertainment mean to you? (50) (LC, OL, 2003, Question B)

- Write about changes you would like to make to your room, **or** to your home, **or** to the area in which you live. (50) (LC, OL, 2002, Question B)

- Imagine you are a radio or TV commentator for a sporting or non-sporting event. Write the commentary you would give on one important moment during that event. (50) (LC, OL, 2002, Question B)

- Imagine you were asked to give an interview during your final term in school. Write the answers you would give to questions 1 and 2 of the interview with Sarah. (50) (LC, OL, 2001, Question B)

## Study Card No.8: How to Write a Successful Description, Commentary or Opinion Piece

● You may be asked to describe or comment on people, places or experiences.

● For these types of description, try to develop an eye for interesting detail. Focus on two or three key aspects of a person, place or event that is interesting or unusual. Do not try to describe everything.

● If describing a person, including yourself, again focus clearly on the aspects of your character or personality that are relevant to the question.

● Many descriptions appeal to our senses: sight, sound, touch and smell. A commentary for a sporting event must bring the game to life for the viewer/listener.

● Well-chosen adjectives and verbs can add drama to your description. A description is really a word-picture; so make the picture as interesting as possible.

● Sometimes, you may have to describe your opinions on a subject. Write clearly and precisely. Do not be tempted to waffle.

● Do not merely write a list of numerous points. It is better to take a small number of points and develop each one fully in a paragraph of its own.

● Language of information is obviously important in any description. However, narrative language (describing/recalling a personal experience), and persuasive language (asking people to accept your point/advice) are also frequently used.

● If your description takes the form of an advertisement, then create an interesting caption or headline, use buzz words that make the product or service appealing, write a slogan, and even consider including a simple logo.

## From the Exam Papers

Read **Question B** below from the 2010 paper. Underline or highlight the key terms of the question. Work out *what* you have to write, *who* you are writing for, and *why* you are writing. These three factors will help you to decide *how* to write your description.

> **5.** Someone had found a white flare but fingers were too cold and stiff to unwrap the tape and light it. Peter struggled trying to turn *Brendan* away but the wind had locked us on what seemed to be a collision course. Then the factory trawler's black bulk slid past us so close that we could make out the welding on the steel plates that towered over us. The lights from her portholes swept over us. We stood looking up at this giant of the sea. She was so close we could reach out and touch her.

**N.B. Candidates may NOT answer Question A and Question B on the same text.**

**Questions A and B carry 50 marks each.**

**Question A**

(i) In your opinion, what were the **three** greatest difficulties faced by Tim Severin and his crew? Explain your answer with reference to the text. (15)

(ii) In paragraphs 4 and 5 how does Tim Severin convey the atmosphere of tension and fear on *Brendan* as the huge factory ship came towards them? (15)

(iii) From your reading of the passage do you think Tim Severin and his crew were brave or foolish or both to undertake their voyage? Give reasons for your answer. (20)

**Question B**

A competition has been announced to select crew members for a new *Brendan* voyage. In approximately 250 words explain to Tim Severin why you should be chosen as a crew member for this voyage. (50)

Page 5 of 12

*Who?* You are writing to **Tim Severin.**

*What?* Write a **description**.

*Why?* You are writing to **explain why you should be chosen** as a crew member for a new *Brendan* voyage.

## Student's Answer Plan – Five Short Paragraphs

● Introduction – introduce myself, what I want to say.

● Paragraph 2 – background information.

● Paragraph 3 – why I would be a good crew member – describe my qualities as a sailor.

- Paragraph 4 – show awareness of background/significance of voyage.

- Paragraph 5 – explain what I can offer the voyage – total commitment.

- Conclusion – hopeful of success.

**Note on language:** Use formal language. All categories possible but begin with information and follow through with persuasion.

## ◯ Sample Answer to Question B

FAO: Mr Tim Severin

Hello Tim. Let me introduce myself. My name is Sarah Jane Cooper and I am writing to you in relation to your search for crew members for a new Brendan voyage.

I am 17 years of age and I live in Wexford town. All my life I have been fascinated by sailing boats. My first experience of the sea occurred when I was only four years old and my mum and dad took me sailing off the west coast of Ireland. Over the years, I have grown to love sailing more and more. The sea is a magical place for me and even though I am only 17, I feel I am already drawn towards her mystery, her power and her magic.

I have completed several training courses in sailing over the summer months and won a special merit award for my seamanship at a sailing school in Dungarvan last summer. I am technically skilled at sailing, therefore, but I am also a good team player. I know how important teamwork would be on a Brendan voyage and I am confident I can play my part.

A new Brendan voyage would be an exciting and challenging experience for me. To sail across the Atlantic on what is essentially a patchwork quilt stretched over a wooden frame would be amazing! I would just love to work with other sailors to recreate the sailing achievements of St Brendan hundreds of years before.

This is a unique challenge and an adventure that would bring out the best in me. I can guarantee you a 100 per cent commitment to the project on my part and I can assure you that you would not regret accepting me as a crew member.

Thank you for your time and I hope to hear from you soon.

Sarah Jane Cooper

## Answering Techniques

- **Introduce yourself** and explain why you are writing.

- Describe your background. Only include relevant details. Tim Severin does not want to know if you are good at skateboarding!

- List any qualifications you may have. Explain what you can bring to the voyage.

- This student cleverly uses information from the comprehending text – it would impress Tim that you know a bit about the boat and its history.

- Use **persuasive phrases** to make your case stronger, e.g. 'I can guarantee you . . .', or 'I can assure you . . .' This helps to **inspire confidence** in your ability.

- Close in a warm, friendly manner.

- Word count is 298 – around 250 is mentioned in the question, so this is fine.

# Write a Diary or Blog

## What Kind of Questions to Expect

Here are some of the questions on diaries from past exam papers:

- Imagine you have been successful at one of the following: (i) achieving a sporting ambition; (ii) overcoming a fear or phobia; (iii) participating in a school play, musical or debate. Write three diary entries related to this achievement. (50) (LC, OL, 2012, Question B)

- You have won a competition entitled 'Be a Celebrity for a Day'. Write out **two diary entries** or **two blog entries** about your experience. (50) (LC, OL, 2009, Question B)

- Imagine you are Lashly. Write **two** diary entries describing your thoughts as you wait to be rescued. (50) (LC, OL, 2007, Question B)

- A Prisoner's Diary. Imagine you have been sentenced to life in prison. Write a diary entry for **each** of your first three days as a prisoner. (50) (LC, OL, 2005, Question B)

- Imagine you are one of the people in Text 3. Write **three short diary entries** covering a week in your life. (50) (LC, OL, 2004, Question B)

- Old money – new money! Write two or three diary entries recording your own or your family's experiences during the first week of the changeover to the euro. (50) (LC, OL, 2002, Question B)

## Study Card No.9: How to Write a Successful Diary

- In a diary entry question, you may be asked to describe **your thoughts and feelings** on a particular topic, event, or experience.

- Write the **date** at the top of your diary entry.

- You may begin with a **simple opening**, such as 'Dear Diary', or alternatively use any imaginative name you have for your diary.

- Give your diary a **personal ring** by including phrases such as 'I believe', 'I think', 'I felt', 'it amazed me that . . .' and so on. You may also use casual phrases such as 'no way!', 'eh, hello out there!', 'wow!', where appropriate.

- Contractions may also be used (e.g. 'I've', 'won't', 'they've') to make it sound more realistic.

- When you describe an event or special occasion, always give **your reaction** to that event after describing what happened.

- Many diary entries include information on the **5Ws** and **H**. For any event or experience, you may be able to describe *what* happened, *where* it happened, *when* it happened, *who* was there, *why* did it happen, and *how* it happened. Then explain in detail your reactions to and feelings on these.

- Sometimes you might like to describe how an event changed you in some way. Did you see things differently after the event? Did it surprise or shock you? Did you learn something new from the event and so on?

- The tone is important in a diary. If you are recording a celebration, create a tone of delight and joy by using positive, upbeat words and phrases.

- You may include simple drawings, sketches or images in a private diary.

- Remember that the language in a diary may be chatty, colloquial, informal and casual, but not offensive.

## Study Card No.10: How to Write a Successful Blog

- **A blog** – short for a web log – is a type of digital diary.

- While a diary is often written for your eyes only, a blog, however, is posted onto the internet where perhaps thousands of people may read it. The audience, therefore, for a diary is a **private one**, while for a blog it is a **public audience**.

- Also, a blog may have many authors, each one logging on and posting their own contributions.

- In this way, **a blog post is a little like having a conversation**, with a chain of blogs and responses being posted on any one topic.

- What you say, and how you say it, is what makes an interesting blog. Begin your blog with a title. Blog titles should be short, simple and catchy. An interesting title will grab the attention of your readers.

- In your opening lines, hook your readers with interesting, dramatic or controversial content.

- Blogs are about you. Write about your day, your thoughts, your fears and so on. Read the question carefully, this will give a clear focus and purpose to your writing.

- Keep your ideas short and to the point. **Do not waffle**.

- In your conclusion, ask your readers a question. This would encourage them to respond to your blog and emphasises that a blog is written for a public audience.

## From the Exam Papers

Read **Question B** below from the 2009 paper. Underline or highlight the key terms of the question. Work out what you have to write, *who* you are writing for, and *why* you are writing. These three factors will help you to decide *how* to write your diary.

Make a plan and then write your diary. Compare your diary with the sample diary on page 89.

---

*Q4.  How do you protect your website from misuse?*
We are fully aware that the website has the potential to be dangerous. We have made it clear what's acceptable to put on YouTube and what's not. Content that is violent or hateful or generally unsuitable we can remove in a matter of minutes.

*Q5.   What does the future hold for YouTube?*
People are always going to want quality information and entertainment be it from newspapers, television or magazines and certainly that demand is not going to disappear. YouTube is adding to the choice. We are continuing to work on our website which is still so young. The speed  of connection to the website will continue to improve.  It will be increasingly possible to connect from wherever you are at any time. It's a chance for different cultures to talk to each other. Every day YouTube gets bigger and as a result I'm working harder!

---

**N.B.  Candidates may NOT answer Question A and Question B on the same text.**

**Questions A and B carry 50 marks each.**

**Question A**

(i)   Having read the entire interview, what do you think are the advantages and disadvantages of YouTube?  Support your answer with reference to the text.     (15)

(ii)  The picture that accompanies this text shows YouTube inventor Chad Hurley, Planet Earth and computer screens. Do you think this is a suitable picture to accompany the interview?  Give reasons for your answer.     (15)

(iii) In this interview, what does Chad Hurley tell us about the public's response to the development of YouTube?     (20)

**Question B**

You have won a competition entitled 'Be a Celebrity for a Day'.  Write out **two diary entries** or **two blog entries** about your experience.     (50)

Page 3 of 8 ➡

---

*What?* You are writing **two** diary entries OR **two** blog entries.

*Who?* A personal diary is written for you only (private audience). A blog, however, may be read by thousands online (public audience).

*Why?* You are writing about your experience (description and reaction) of being a celebrity for a day.

## Student's Answer Plan

- **Entry 1 - Diary**
  - Dramatic opening – catch excitement of winning.
  - Tell my friends – texting all day.

- **Entry 2**
  - Collected at 8 a.m. by limo.
  - Private jet.
  - X-Factor, then shopping.
  - West End show.
  - Autographs.
  - Home and exhausted.

## Sample Answer to Question B

15 December

Dear Diary,

I cannot believe it, I just cannot believe it! Today I got the most amazing text message I have ever received in my life. I've won the Celeb for a Day Competition. I actually won it, it's crazy, completely mad!

There I was in the school canteen with Tom and Linda, chewing on an apple and the same old predictable conversations – dreading another weekend with no money and nowhere to go.

Suddenly, my phone bleeped. In a second, my face changed from the gloomy and glum look to the shock and elation look! Linda thought I had won the lotto! But it was better than that!

Spent the rest of the day (at the back of music class, and double science) texting my friends. I'm sure they'll be mad jealous! At least I hope they will!!

16 December

Dear Diary,

Today was the best day of my life, bar none! A white limo pulled up outside my place at 9 this morning. You should have seen the look on the neighbours' faces, peering around half-opened blinds. Within an hour, I was in Dublin airport and boarding a private jet to London to meet the X-factor team. Simon wanted me to help judge some of the acts in the qualifying rounds! I had to sit in Cheryl Cole's seat. Can you believe it! Me, taking Cheryl Cole's place. Wicked!

For lunch, we were whisked off to a posh restaurant in central London.

Afterwards, Simon handed me an envelope from Cheryl. It was a shopping voucher for €5,000 for Harrods! Can things get any better? I was thrilled.

After many hours trying so hard to blow my 'pocket money', Louis arranged for me to meet some of the cast of 'Cats' in the West End. The show was amazing; the lights and costumes, the singing and dancing were really out of this world. (I'm never going to doss in music class again.) Backstage, I got loads of autographs and even Andrew Lloyd Weber signed my souvenir T-shirt. How cool is that!

At 2 a.m., I arrived back at Dublin, exhausted and a bit dazed by it all. But what a truly incredible day. I just do not know how celebs can do it every day. Who knows, someday I think I could get used to it! Now, where's my apple?

## Answering Techniques

- In a diary, your language can be more **casual and chatty** than normal. A relaxed use of language is typical of the register of a personal diary and will be awarded high marks.

- Set the scene. Describe how you got the news and how you reacted to it.

- Small sketches or drawings may be used, but do not overdo it.

- Do not focus solely on describing your special day; capturing your **reactions** to what happened is just as important in a diary.

# Write a Personal Letter

## ◐ What Kind of Questions to Expect

Here are some of the questions on personal letters from past exam papers:

- Imagine you are the young Peter Sheridan. Write the letter he might have written to his grandmother describing the events that took place in his house on New Year's Eve, 1959 and his role in them. (50) (LC, OL, 2009, Question B)

● Imagine Della writes to the problem page of a magazine asking if she should sell her hair to buy Jim a present. Write the letter of advice that the problem page would send to Della. (50) (LC, OL, 2004, Question B)

## Study Card No.11: How to Write a Personal Letter

● Having read your question carefully, make sure you are clear about your:
  - **Subject**: *what* you are writing about.
  - **Audience**: *who* you are writing for.
  - **Purpose**: *why* you are writing.

● Most personal letters are written to share your ideas, feelings and experiences with a close friend or family member.

● Personal letters may also be written to congratulate a friend on an achievement or important occasion, or to offer advice. Depending on why you are writing, the tone of your letter may be warm and friendly, or perhaps respectful and courteous.

● Aim to write three or four paragraphs, or more if you decide to use short paragraphs.

● Begin by saying why you are writing. Then share your information, tell your story and describe your feelings. Usually, you can use conversational, relaxed expressions in a personal letter.

● The main language used will be informative. You will also use narrative language as you keep the person up to date on recent events.

● Keep your descriptions clear and to the point. Do not wander off the purpose of your letter. Refer back to your answer plan before you start writing each new paragraph.

● Each key idea should be developed in a paragraph of its own.

● Finish with a brief conclusion. The closure should be informal.

● The language in a personal letter is less formal than, say, in a business letter. Informal phrases such as 'Hi Sandra', 'Take care', 'Look after yourself', 'See you soon' are all appropriate in a personal or informal letter.

## From the Exam Papers

Read the **Question B** below from the 2009 paper. Underline or highlight the key terms of the question. Work out *what* you have to write, *who* you are writing for, and *why* you are writing. These three factors will help you to decide *how* to write your personal letter.

Make a plan and then write your personal letter. Compare your personal letter with the sample answer below.

---

**3.** "There's your problem. There's your problem, right there. The church is blocking your signal," Paddy said to Da. "The church stands directly between you and a perfect picture."

Da saw it immediately.

"The signal is going to hit them houses and bounce over there." Paddy turned the light southwards. "It's going to re-form over there, do a little jazz dance and work its way into us from the direct opposite side."

Paddy turned the light towards me. The two of them shouted at me with one voice.

"Turn it around son, turn it around."

I turned the aerial in the complete opposite direction. Word went down the line. Word came up the line.

– "There's a picture!"
– "There's a picture!"
– "There's a picture!"
– "There's a picture!"

**4.** Half an hour into 1960 we all sat staring at the television. The sound was perfect. A man was describing the celebrations in Trafalgar Square. There was definitely something on the screen. Outlines that looked like human beings. I went right up close but all I could see were dots and lines. Paddy touched something at the back of the set and there it was – a perfect picture. Well, nearly perfect. Lots of snow but a definite picture. We all clapped. It was a woman on a horse. She looked majestic. We stayed glued to the television. The music blared out and the Queen inspected the guard. Da and Paddy stood behind us.

I couldn't wait for the rest of the 1960s to begin.

---

**N.B.  Candidates may NOT answer Question A and Question B on the same text.**

**Questions A and B carry 50 marks each.**

**Question A**

(i)   What do you learn about the Sheridan family from your reading of the extract?  Support your answer with reference to the extract.                    (15)

(ii)  This extract is full of detailed description.
      Choose your favourite detail/description from the passage and explain why you liked it.                    (15)

(iii) How does the writer create an atmosphere of suspense and excitement in paragraph 2 of the extract?                    (20)

**Question B**

Imagine you are the young Peter Sheridan.  Write the **letter** he might have written to his grandmother describing the events that took place in his house on New Year's Eve, 1959 and his role in them.                    (50)

*What?* You are writing a letter (personal).

*Who?* You are Peter Sheridan, writing to your grandmother.

*Why?* You are writing to describe what took place in the house on New Year's Eve.

## Student's Answer Plan

- Shape response as a personal letter – include address, greeting and personal closure.

- Paragraph 1 – ask how granny is and thank her for presents.

- Paragraph 2 – yesterday's events: set the scene, excitement.

- Paragraph 3 –on roof with aerial; throwing snowballs.

- Paragraph 4 – my role: climbing on roof, holding aerial, frozen but brave.

- Paragraph 5 – my first picture: the Queen, amazing.

- Conclusion.

**Note on language**: Use chatty, informative language and, also, some narrative with description. Keep tone warm and friendly.

## Sample Answer to Question B

> 44 Seville Place,
>
> Dublin.
>
> 1 January 1960
>
> Dear Granny,
>
> I hope you are keeping well. I'm sorry for not writing since last September. Thanks for the two pounds when I went back to school back then. The new socks you bought me for Christmas are lovely and warm.
>
> Yesterday was a very exciting day, Granny. When I saw the first snowflakes falling I just knew it was going to be a brilliant day! And then, guess what happened? Da walked in the door at around 4 o'clock with a television set! He said we'd be able to watch pictures within an hour! Johnny, Shea and Rita jumped up and down with excitement. I wasn't sure what all the fuss was about, I mean to me it was just a big, black box. Ma told them to quieten down or they'd waken little Frankie.
>
> But then Grandma, the fun really started. Da and Uncle Paddy headed up on the roof with an aerial. They were frozen. They had such trouble trying to find a picture. They must have been on the roof for hours. I stood in the front garden throwing my last few snowballs onto the roof as darkness started to fall.
>
> Da rigged up a light then. It threw huge shadows over the snow. Inside we all huddled around the mysterious box and stared at a little white dot, then some snow. But, there was no picture. Then Da had one of his bright ideas. And yeah, it meant I had to crawl up on the roof to hold the aerial. Gran, I was absolutely frozen. I don't want you feeling sorry for me, but I was really scared up on that roof. Ma said I was very brave and deserve something special.

Anyway, I turned the aerial one way, then another and suddenly everyone cried out, 'There's a picture, there's a picture!' I was so proud! I raced into the kitchen, at nearly one o'clock in the morning, cold but excited. Eight hours after the television arrived, I saw for the very first time a television picture. It wasn't that clear, but I saw it. My very first television picture. I saw the Queen. Oh, you should have seen her, Gran, you would have loved it. If you come over before I go back to school, I can show you how it works.

Until then, Gran, I hope you've a very happy 1960. I wish I didn't have to go back to school. But then, I'm happy because I have the best and most generous Granny in the world!

Lots of love,
Brave Peter

## Answering Techniques

- Use the layout of a personal letter. Your address is in the top right-hand corner.
- Skip a line after your address and write out a date.
- The greeting shows the boy's respect for his grandmother.
- Explain briefly why you are writing the letter. This should take no more than a few lines.
- Use ideas, names and descriptions from Text 2 – the Family's First Television – to help you.
- Tell the story in a chatty, friendly way. Use paragraphs.
- Choose words (especially adjectives and verbs) carefully to describe what happened and how you felt.
- Invite your grandma over to see the TV. Note use of contractions.
- Personal, warm closure. Finish with your signature.

# Write a Formal Letter

## What Kind of Questions to Expect

Here are some of the questions on formal letters from past exam papers:

- Write a letter to cartoonist, Gary Larson, in which you outline your response to the cartoon that appears in Image 2, on page five. (50) (LC, OL, 2013, Question B)

- Write a letter to former President McAleese in which you express your own hopes for Ireland in the future. (50) (LC, OL, 2012, Question B)

- Imagine NASA (The National Aeronautics and Space Administration) has advertised looking for a young person to be part of their next moon mission. Write a letter of application emphasising your suitability for a position on the team. (50) (LC, OL, 2011, Question B)

- Imagine that you live beside the 'neighbours from hell'. Write the letter you would send to the police complaining about this problem. (50) (LC, OL, 2008, Question B)

- Write a letter to your favourite pop star or celebrity inviting him or her to come to the launch of a charity to help the homeless. In your letter, you should explain how you intend to raise money for the charity. (50) (LC, OL, 2003, Question B)

- Imagine you are the writer of Text 2. Write a letter to the owner of the 'computerised hotel' complaining about your experience. (50) (LC, OL, 2001, Question B)

## Study Card No.12: How to Write a Successful Formal Letter

- Having read your question carefully, make sure you are clear about your:
  - **Subject**: *what* you are writing about.
  - **Audience**: *who* you are writing for.
  - **Purpose**: *why* you are writing.
- Formal letters include those which:
  - Make a complaint or request.
  - Invite someone to a formal event.
  - Communicate opinions with a newspaper editor, or with some famous person.
  - Apply for a job.
- Remember to use the appropriate shape/structure for your letter: include your address (make one up!) and the recipient's address (see sample answer next).
- Aim to write around four to five paragraphs. Include in this your reason for writing (paragraph 1), the main points or comments you wish to make (paragraphs 2, 3 and 4), and a conclusion (paragraph 5).
- Sometimes, you may have to use the language of argument or persuasion.
- Support your points with facts, statistics and personal anecdotes.
- Each paragraph can be quite short, e.g. two or three sentences. Start a new paragraph for each new point.
- Begin each new paragraph with a linking phrase such as: 'Furthermore', 'In addition' or 'Another'.
- In your final paragraph, write down what action you expect to be taken, or what response you expect.
- While the tone may be firm or businesslike, remain polite. Never use abusive or offensive language.
- Use contractions such as 'I'm', and 'I've' sparingly. Better to use 'I am' and 'I have' to create a more impersonal tone. However, contractions can help to create a warmer tone which might be required in some formal letters.
- Write in a clear, concise style. Avoid long, rambling sentences. Do not use clichés or slang.

## From the Exam Papers

Read the **Question B** below from the 2011 paper. Underline or highlight the key terms of the question. Work out *what* you have to write, *who* you are writing for, and *why* you are writing. These three factors will help you to decide *how* to write your formal letter.

Make a plan and then write your formal letter. Compare your formal letter with the sample answer below.

> Apollo 1 rocket. For fifteen minutes I stood on that walkway and enjoyed the peace and solitude as I contemplated the journey ahead. I recalled just how wonderful my life had been to get me to this point. We had trained, simulated and tested nearly every element of the mission. But there were no guarantees. Even with all the preparation, so many things could go wrong. As astronauts, we were trained to accept such risks, even the risk of not returning. But I had to put these concerns aside and climb aboard the spacecraft.
>
> **5.** "Two, One … Zero …" The normally calm voice of Public Affairs Officer Jack King cracked with emotion from the Control Room. "All engines running!" In front of us what looked like hundreds of tiny amber lights blinked on the instrument panels.
>
> Inside the spacecraft we could hear the mighty rumble as the controlled but excited voice cried, "Liftoff! We have liftoff!" The rumbling sound grew louder and the huge rocket felt as though it swayed slightly as it smoothly inched off the pad.
>
> **6.** Large shards of frost fell from the sleek metal sides as the blue sky seemed to move past the hatch window directly above me. Below us an inferno of flames, steam and gases blazed all around the launch-pad. With 7.6 million pounds of thrust pushing all 3,240 tons of rocket and spacecraft, we cleared the tower and rapidly accelerated, the g-forces dramatically building up and pressing against us. We were on our way to the moon!

**N.B. Candidates may NOT answer Question A and Question B on the same text.**

**Questions A and B carry 50 marks each.**

**Question A**

(i) What impression of Buzz Aldrin do you form from reading this text? Support your answer with reference to the text. (15)

(ii) From what you have read in the above passage, explain why you would or would not like to have joined Buzz Aldrin on his way to the moon. Give reasons for your answer. (15)

(iii) (a) Suggest three words or phrases, of your own or from the passage, that you think capture the atmosphere before the launch of the Apollo 11 rocket. Explain your choices.

(b) Describe an image (photo, painting, drawing, etc.) that could be used to illustrate this extract, which would capture the atmosphere you described in (a) above. (20)

**Question B**

Imagine NASA (The National Aeronautics and Space Administration) has advertised looking for a young person to be part of their next moon mission. Write a **letter of application** emphasising your suitability for a position on the team. (50)

*Page 3 of 12* ➡

*What?* You are writing a letter (formal).

*Who?* It is for NASA – formal audience

*Why?* You are applying for a place on a moon mission, emphasising why you are a suitable candidate.

## Student's Answer Plan

- Shape response as a letter – include addresses, formal greeting and closure.
- Paragraph 1- say who I am.
- Paragraph 2 – briefly mention why I admire NASA.
- Paragraph 3 – first reason – personal fitness.
- Paragraph 4 – second reason – mental strength – studying Physics.
- Paragraph 5 – third reason – make the dream a reality.
- Closure – express thanks for considering application.

**Note on language**: Formal language throughout – information, narration and persuasion.

## Sample Answer to Question B

> 11 Oak Heights,
> Drumshannon,
> Co. Offaly.
>
> 1 March
>
> Mr Randolph King,
> Head of Recruitment,
> Kennedy Space Centre,
> Florida,
> United States of America.
>
> Dear Mr King,
>
> My name is David Larkin and I am an 18-year-old student from Co. Offaly in Ireland. I have recently discovered that NASA is recruiting young people to be part of your next space mission to the moon and I would be honoured if you would consider my application.
>
> I have admired the remarkable achievements of NASA and its astronauts for several years now. From Apollo 11 to the adventures of the Lunar Rover, I have watched, with a mixture of awe and fascination, the remarkable exploration and research that has catapulted humankind into space and beyond.
>
> I would dearly love to become a part of the NASA story, to make my small contribution to exploration and discovery. Let me suggest why I might be an ideal candidate.
>
> Firstly, I understand that to be an astronaut you must be in peak physical condition. I have been attending our local gym three times a week over the past two years and have reached a level of personal fitness that would serve me well on your mission. I also play on the local rugby team where I have been complimented on my stamina, dedication and courage in both competition and in training matches. Sport has also taught me the importance of team-work and I'm sure that being an effective team-player is vitally important on this moon mission.

Another area that is important would be my mental strength. While I am no genius, and I do not have a Masters Degree in Aeronautical Engineering, I am currently studying for my Leaving Certificate in Ireland where I will sit four Higher Level and three Ordinary Level Papers. My favourite subject in school is Physics. I enjoy the challenge of problem-solving and I am confident that I can go on to third level college to further my studies in this area. Space would be like another laboratory to me – a fascinating place where I would relish the opportunity to conduct experiments on board the shuttle.

Finally, I must add that I have always been an enthusiastic follower of NASA and its missions. Indeed, I have read that your own father, Mr Jack King, announced to the world that Apollo 11 had lifted off the launch pad back in 1969. I'm sure he was a huge influence on you when you were younger. When I was younger, I used to cut up boxes and cover them in tin-foil and imagine I was on a space mission while crawling through a tiny porthole. I remember that at one time I refused to eat my meals unless they were served through the 'service hatch' of my space craft to be eaten inside. At night, I would find myself staring at the moon, telescope in one hand, map in the other, imagining, dreaming that maybe one day, just maybe. . . You see, I have dreamed the dream. Now I want to make it a reality.

May I thank you for taking the time to read my letter. NASA has always been an inspiration to me. I can assure you that I would be as devoted and passionate in a mission to the moon as the heroes who first conquered space in 1969. Like Armstrong, Collins and Buzz himself, I will not shy away from the challenge. Rather, I will stand tall and give this mission my very best, not because it is easy, but, as your former President Kennedy said: 'because it is hard'.

Yours sincerely,
David Larkin

## Answering Techniques

- Use the layout of a formal letter, including both the sender's and the recipient's addresses.
- Use a formal greeting.
- Explain briefly why you are writing the letter. This should take no more than a few lines.
- Give some details to show you know something about the work of NASA.
- Note that tone is confident and optimistic without being boastful or arrogant.
- Keep each paragraph focused on the task – why you are suitable.
- Note the mix of information, narration and persuasion in the answer – an effective combination.
- Writer is courteous at all times.
- Note how the writer cleverly makes use of the information mentioned in the reading text.

- Formal closure. 'Yours sincerely' when you open the letter with the person's name. 'Yours faithfully' when you begin a letter with 'Dear Sir or Madam'.

- Finish with your signature.

# Write a Feature Article

## For a School Magazine or Newspaper

### What Kind of Questions to Expect

Here are a couple of the questions on feature articles from past exam papers:

- **A Feature Article**
  Write a feature article for a daily newspaper entitled: 'Staying Fit and Healthy'. (50) (LC, OL, 2007, Question B)

- **Computer games** – do they have a good or a bad effect on young people? Write an article for a newspaper expressing your view on this question. (50) (LC, OL, 2001, Question B)

> **Study Card No.13:** How to Write a Successful Feature Article for a Magazine or Newspaper
>
> - Having read your question carefully, make sure you are clear about your:
>   - **Subject**: *what* you are writing about.
>   - **Audience**: *who* you are writing for.
>   - **Purpose**: *why* you are writing.
> - A feature article contains information on a particular issue, place or even person. Sometimes feature articles include some background analysis of the story.
> - Many feature articles include the opinion or advice of the writer. The main thing is that a feature article, while informative, should be entertaining and interesting.
> - In the exam, therefore, you may include your own opinions on topics of interest to the public – underage drinking, violence on our streets, and so on. Read the question carefully. If you do not have strong views on the issue in the question, perhaps consider taking a different Question B.
> - The tone of a feature article should be personal. The reader should get a sense of the writer's own stand on an issue. If you are instructed to write for a school magazine, your language, vocabulary and tone (also known as register) may be more relaxed and chatty than say an article for a broadsheet newspaper.

- The article often begins with information, but then more persuasion is used as the writer expresses personal viewpoints.

- Refer to a personal experience to make your article more interesting and convincing. Anecdotes can be very persuasive.

- If you are trying to prove a point, use facts, statistics (you can make them up!) or quotations from famous people to support your points.

- Remember to shape your ideas correctly.

  - Create an interesting headline.

  - Next, include a by-line (make up your name as the journalist writing the article).

  - Your opening sentence should act like a 'hook' and draw readers in. Make it dramatic, interesting or unusual.

  - Usually you would answer the 5Ws and H early on in paragraphs 1 and 2. However, you have the option in a feature of leaving some information until later in the article. Use link words between each paragraph such as: 'However', 'Another', 'While', 'Although' and 'Later'.

  - You may use sub-headlines to make your article look like a real newspaper article.

  - Continue your article with your own opinions.

- Your conclusion/last paragraph is very important. Use it to summarise the key point(s) of the article. Make sure it focuses directly on the key instructions in the question.

# Write a Newspaper Report

### ◉ What Kind of Questions to Expect

Here are some of the questions on newspaper reports from past exam papers:

- Imagine you are a journalist reporting on one of the events featured in Text 3. Write your report. (50) (LC, OL, 2007, Question B)

- **You Were There! – A Newspaper Report**
  Imagine you are a newspaper reporter on the island with Phyl and Mike. Based on some of the events in the extract, write a newspaper report. (50) (LC, OL, 2006, Question B)

● Imagine you are a newspaper reporter with a tabloid newspaper. You have been sent to report the story behind one of the images or predictions. Write the headline you would use and a short exciting report. (150–200 words). (50) (LC, OL, 2001, Question B)

## Study Card No.14: How to Write a Successful Newspaper Report

● Having read your question carefully, make sure you are clear about your:
  - **Subject**: *what* you are writing about.
  - **Audience**: *who* you are writing for.
  - **Purpose**: *why* you are writing.

● Write in the register of a newspaper report. You must, therefore, include the language of information and create an impersonal tone.

● Remember, your main focus in writing a news report, whether it be for a newspaper, website or radio programme, is to provide factual information. You do not have to try to persuade the readers/listeners that certain facts are true.

● Nonetheless, sometimes you may want to include different viewpoints in your news story. For example, if you were writing a sports news report, you might include two different opinions from both football managers on a disputed penalty in extra time.

● Begin with a headline that will grab the reader's attention. Beneath that, write out a by-line (who the report is written by).

● Your readers will want to know, early on, the 5Ws and H of your news report: *what* happened, *who* was involved, *when* did it happen, *where* did it happen, *why* did it happen and *how* did it happen.

● All of the answers to these questions should appear in the opening one or two paragraphs of your article. The opening paragraph is called your lead paragraph. It really is a brief summary of your story.

● You can then include more details in the remaining paragraphs. Use quotes from people involved in the story, or briefly describe some eyewitness accounts of what happened.

● Remember, start a new paragraph for a new point. Newspaper paragraphs are usually quite short – often one, two or three sentences.

● Use sub-headings if you wish, to give your report the 'look' of a newspaper article. A sub-heading should indicate, in two or three words, the main point of the paragraph.

● Use clear and concise language. Reread your article to make sure it makes sense and check for accurate punctuation and spelling.

# Write a Review

## ◉ What Kind of Questions to Expect

Here are some of the questions on reviews from past exam papers:

● Write a review for your school magazine of one of the following: a funny film or TV show; an amusing book or a live comedy performance. (50) (LC, OL, 2013, Question B)

● **Review**
Write a review for your school magazine of any film that you have enjoyed. Your review should encourage other students to go and see it. (50) (LC, OL, 2006, Question B)

● Write a review of your favourite film or TV programme or radio programme. (50) (LC, OL, 2003, Question B)

## Study Card No.15: How to Write a Successful Review

● Having read your question carefully, make sure you are clear about your:
  • **Subject**: *what* you are writing about.
  • **Audience**: *who* you are writing for.
  • **Purpose**: *why* you are writing.

● You may be asked to write a review, for example, of a favourite television programme, a film, a drama, a concert, a radio programme, a book, a CD or DVD, or a favourite website.

● Much of a review is written using the language of information.

● Make sure the information you write is relevant and of interest to your audience.

● You may also use persuasion, where you try to persuade your reader to see a movie, read a book or attend a concert.

- You should try to write your review using the following structure or shape:
  - Begin with an introduction; introduce briefly the subject of your review. Who wrote the book, directed the film, starred in the drama?
  - In paragraph 2, write down some factual information about the subject. Perhaps give a brief plot outline of a film or novel (but do not reveal the ending!), or set the scene for a concert.
  - In paragraph 3, give your analysis and opinions: was it well written/ performed/produced; what were the highlights or lowlights. If you want to be critical of some aspect, give reasons for your opinion.
  - Avoid using general adjectives such as 'good', 'great', 'poor', and 'OK'. Be more precise, e.g. use entertaining, shocking, surprising, riveting, inspiring, gripping, or disappointing.
  - Finally, conclude with your **recommendation**. Do you think others would enjoy/benefit from reading the book, seeing the film, viewing the website? Give three reasons why. Finish with a star rating, out of five. For example, 3/5 might look like this: ★★★☆☆

## From the Exam Papers

Read the **Question B** below from the 2013 paper. Underline or highlight the key terms of the question. Work out *what* you have to write, *who* you are writing for, and *why* you are writing. These three factors will help you to decide *how* to write your review.

Make a plan and then write your review. Compare your review with the sample answer below.

5.    Wednesday night was my big night. My five minutes of jokes were spinning round and round in my head. I went with my sister and her boyfriend. When we arrived at the club I thought I might vomit. The Wednesday new-act night had free entry, so the audience was packed with people who didn't like to pay for entertainment. I kept rehearsing my act, the keywords of which I had scribbled on my hand. I was on third. Daniel Kitson was again hosting and was just as hilarious as the previous week. He was enjoying himself and doing far too long between the acts. The audience were in the palm of his biro-free hand. He would introduce each act almost as if he was apologizing for the interruption to the Daniel Kitson Show, and it wasn't an interruption the audience appreciated because he was significantly funnier than everybody else. He took out the list of acts from his pocket and read out my name, beginning my comedy career. The audience applauded as I walked towards the stage and took the microphone out of its stand. The view from the stage was surreal. Nothing can prepare you for all the expectant faces staring at you. I can't remember what I opened with but I remember hearing the sound of laughter. It was amazing. 'I'm a natural,' I thought, 'this is a breeze.' Unfortunately, I then proceeded to struggle for the next four and a half minutes. I walked off-stage to lacklustre applause.

6.    Technically the gig was a disaster, but I did get one laugh, one solitary laugh, something to build on. I was so relieved that it was over and proud that I had cleared the most terrifying hurdle of my life so far. I had sat in the audience at the Comedy Store confident in my ability to succeed as a stand-up, but now I knew that was because the comedians made it look easy. It wasn't. I had been bitten by the comedy bug.

*This text has been adapted, for the purpose of assessment, without the author's prior consent.*

**N.B. Candidates may NOT answer Question A and Question B on the same text.**

**Questions A and B carry 50 marks each.**

**Question A**

(i)    Based on what you have read in the above passage, what qualities and abilities does the writer possess that may have helped him to become a successful stand-up comedian? Explain your answer with reference to the extract.                    (15)

(ii)   From what Michael McIntyre has written, what impression do you form of comedy-show host, Daniel Kitson? Support your answer with reference to the text.  (15)

(iii)  (a)   Explain why **any two** of the following words could be used to describe the writer's first night as a stand-up comedian at the Comedy Café.

       Successful       Disastrous       Nerve-wracking

       Support your answer with reference to the text.                    (10)

       (b)   Based on what you have read in the above extract, would you like to read more of Michael McIntyre's book, *Life and Laughing*? Explain your answer with reference to the extract.                    (10)

**Question B**

Write a **review** for your school magazine of **one** of the following: a funny film or TV show; an amusing book or a live comedy performance.                    (50)

*What?* You are writing a review.

*Who?* The audience is your peers as your review will be published in a school magazine.

*Why?* You are writing to give an assessment of a funny film/TV show/book/live performance.

## Student's Answer Plan

- Shape response as a review.
- Paragraph 1 – information- briefly tell the story.
- Paragraph 2 – analysis of key aspects – give opinions here.
- Paragraph 3 – consider opinions of other reviewers.
- Paragraph 4 – recommendation – comment on why I think students should watch the film.

**Note on language**: Written for peers, so more relaxed, informal language. Include information and persuasion.

## Sample Answer to Question B

### The School Review

### Born a Brown - Mrs Brown and her boys
By Saoirse Hunter, 6th Year

Welcome back students and I hope you all enjoyed a great Easter. See any good movies or tv programmes over the holiday break, or too busy revising for exams? Well, give yourself a well-earned break and check out the hilarious new series of Mrs Brown's Boys starring our very own Brendan O'Carroll. I sat down to watch the latest episode with my gran on Saturday last and I thought I'd die laughing!

Episode One in the third series is called 'New Mammy' and centres on the arrival of Mrs Brown's newly-born grandchildren to Maria. The episode has the usual mix of conflict, chaos and commotion between family members and lovers. Meanwhile, despite all the drama unfolding in the Dublin family home, Grandad's only concern is that he 'can't see the 'telly'!

The star of the show is undoubtedly Agnes Brown, played by Brendan O'Carroll. The series, which is written by O'Carroll, has received rave reviews throughout Ireland and has catapulted O'Carroll's creation onto millions of television screen all over Ireland, the UK and beyond.

The show is filled with one-line gags, most of which are hilarious. This is situational comedy at its best and the scene in Foley's pub where Agnes fills Maria's posh mum Mrs Nicolson with drink is hysterical. Mrs Brown does not hold back on language, however, so be warned that you can expect quite a dose of swearing from the lovable mammy.

I really enjoyed the unscripted moments in the show where, for example, Rory, Mrs Brown's son, explodes into laughter, out-of-character, at the antics of his co-actor O'Carroll. There is another amusing scene when the phone rings in the living room and Agnes answers it before saying it was for one of the camera men on the set who is actually filming the show.

> Overall, I can highly recommend Mrs Brown and her family for a good laugh. The swearing might make it unsuitable for younger viewers (my gran didn't seem to mind!) and some of the gags are laced with sexual innuendo. However, O'Carroll and the rest of the cast give it everything and draw the viewers brilliantly into the story with some terrific performances by Buster, the local rogue, and Mrs Nicolson, our 'sherry trifle'. These are characters we laugh with, but also feel for. At the end of the day, it's all a bit of fun. Not too taxing on the brain, but so what . . . perhaps it's just the break you need from your exam studies! It's complete mayhem and you can catch it on BBC 1 on Saturday evenings at 10pm. Tune in!

## Answering Techniques

- Audience is the student's own peers. Casual opening makes connection.

- Identify the TV programme – add some background information. You can, of course, make up this in the exam – be creative when you have to!

- Name principal cast members/stars.

- After beginning with some information, move on to some analysis of the programme – what happens and why is it funny.

- Don't summarise the complete plot of the show! Answer the question and stay focused on your purpose – this is a positive review overall.

- Point out favourite scenes/characters.

- Finally, you can decide to recommend (or not) the comedy programme. Give two or three clear reasons why the readers of the school magazine might enjoy it.

# Write a Formal Report

## What Kind of Questions to Expect

Here is an example of the questions on formal reports in past exam papers:

- **Greater Freedom for Students**
  Write a report to your school principal suggesting ways in which more freedom could be given to senior students in your school. (50) (LC, OL, 2005, Question B)

## Study Card No.16: How to Write a Successful Report

● Having read your question carefully, make sure you are clear about your:
- **Subject**: *what* you are writing about.
- **Audience**: *who* you are writing for.
- **Purpose**: *why* you are writing.

● A report should include information on a subject or issue. You can, of course, invent this information in your exam answer.

● Use accurate, concise language. Avoid using emotive language – keep it factual. Focus on using the language of information.

● After presenting the facts, draw conclusions and then make some recommendations.

● Do not be biased. However, you can give some of your own opinions in the conclusion, but they must be based on the findings presented earlier in the report.

● When you are writing a report, use the following structure or shape to your answer:
- Give the report a **title**.
- **Introduce the subject** of the report. Also mention who requested the report. Briefly, outline the aims of the report and why it was written.
- In the body of the report, present your **facts** and **findings**.
- You may use **headings** to highlight the key point in each paragraph.
- Conclude with **your own analysis** of the event/situation/incident/problem, based on the findings.
- Finally, make two or three **recommendations**. They should be realistic.
- Sign and date the report.

# Write an Advertisement

## What Kind of Questions to Expect

Here are some of the questions on advertisements from past exam papers:

- **Holiday of a lifetime**
  You work for a company that specialises in activity holidays like bungee-jumping, rock-climbing, going on safari, etc. Write a piece to appear on a webpage promoting an exciting adventure holiday anywhere in the world. (50) (LC, OL, 2010, Question B)

- Imagine you were using **one** of the images 1 to 5 in Text 3 to promote a particular holiday. Write a short advertisement to promote that holiday. (50) (LC, OL, 2005, Question B)

### Study Card No.17: How to Write a Successful Advertisement

- Having read your question carefully, make sure you are clear about your:
  - **Subject**: *what* you are writing about.
  - **Audience**: *who* you are writing for.
  - **Purpose**: *why* you are writing.
- Knowing your target audience is extremely important in writing an advertisement.
- The language has to be written to appeal to this target audience. You can use so-called 'brochure-speak' in ads for holidays.
- Use **buzz words** (e.g. delicious, unrivalled, outstanding, remarkable) and **superlatives** (e.g. sunniest location, creamiest butter, cleanest beaches).
- Create a positive impression of the service or location.
- Use bold, or capital letters or colour to highlight key offers, contact numbers, website addresses, and so on.
- Use **imperatives**: 'Book today', 'Call now', 'Log on and save. Hurry!'
- Offer 'Special Discounts' if booked early. Make your target audience feel that they are getting a quality product or service at a bargain price – quality and value!
- Use repetition of key words and phrases.
- Create a **slogan** or catchy phrase. This will make your ad memorable and more persuasive.
- Consider including an **endorsement** from some celebrity who 'uses' the product or service (e.g. 'Padraig Harrington' eats Flora) or from an expert in the field (e.g. a dentist recommending a new brand of toothpaste).

# Key Exam Tips

## Key Exam Tips and Techniques for Comprehending, Question B

- You only answer one of the Question Bs that appear on the exam paper.

- You may not answer a Question B and a Question A on the same text.

- On your exam paper, write down your time allowance for this question beside the actual question.

- Read the question at least twice. After your first reading, underline the key instructions.

- Then work out exactly what you have to write (e.g. letter, blog or review), who you are writing for (audience) and why you are writing (purpose).

- This will help you to understand how you should write your answer, what kind of language and vocabulary to use and what tone to create (register).

- Once you understand clearly, what the question is instructing you to do, you must plan your answer. This need only take a few minutes, but it is time very well spent.

- In preparing a plan, you may need to use ideas from the comprehending text. Read the text through quickly then tick off a few points that could improve your answer. For a good example of how this is done, see the Sample Answer on writing a personal letter on page 93.

- Look at your plan. Make sure it deals with each part of the question. Start to write your full answer only after completing your plan.

- In writing your answer, remain focused on following the instructions. Do not drift off the point.

- If useful ideas come into your head while in the middle of an answer, you may be able to include these. Your plan, after all, should be flexible.

- Try to give your writing an appropriate shape or structure. For example, if writing a newspaper article, use a headline and by-line. Sub-headings may also be used. At the very least, use paragraphs!

- Do not overwrite. If the question gives no indication of the amount of words to use, for 50 marks, one to one-a-half A4 pages would be fine.

- No matter how much you may 'love' the question, do not write more than two A4 pages. You will need that time to spend on your composing question.

- Remember the key point about **PCLM**: *what* you write is important, but *how* you write will also earn you marks. To get these right, always keep in mind *who* you are writing for and *why* you are writing.

- Write clearly and legibly, and pay attention to accurate spelling and grammar. And – it is worth mentioning again – use paragraphs!

### ◎ Record of What I Have Learned Revising for Paper 1, Section 1, Comprehending, Question B

**Main Tips to Remember When Writing**

● **A talk or speech**

- _____

- _____

- _____

- _____

● **A description**

- _____

- _____

- _____

- _____

● **A diary or blog**

- _____

- _____

- _____

- _____

● **A personal letter**

- _____

- _____

- _____

- _____

● **A formal letter**

- _____

- _____

- _____

- _____

● **A feature article for a newspaper or magazine**

- _____

- _____

- _____

- _____

● **A newspaper report**

   ■ _____

   ■ _____

   ■ _____

   ■ _____

● **A review**

   ■ _____

   ■ _____

   ■ _____

   ■ _____

● **A formal report**

   ■ _____

   ■ _____

   ■ _____

   ■ _____

● **An advertisement**

   ■ _____

   ■ _____

   ■ _____

   ■ _____

## Main things I must remember while answering the functional writing question:

● **Before writing my answer**

   ■ _____

   ■ _____

   ■ _____

   ■ _____

● **While writing my answer**

   ■ _____

   ■ _____

   ■ _____

   ■ _____

● **After writing my answer**

- _____
- _____
- _____
- _____

Well done on completing this section! Our next chapter is about Paper 1, Section 2, Composing.

**Date completed:** _____

# Your Last Minute Revision!

## Around 10 Minutes Revision for Each Study Card

**Revise your Study Cards. You will find these on the following pages:**

### Around 20 Minutes Revision
(for each worked exam paper)

It is a good idea to study again the four key steps to improve your functional writing skills.

- **Step 1**
  Reread the way questions were broken down, underlined/highlighted in this section. Make sure you know what you have to write, who you are writing for, and why you are writing. This will help you to work out how to use language in your answer: what type of vocabulary to use, and what type of tone to create.

- **Step 2**
  Reread the sample answer plans in this section.

- **Step 3**
  Reread the sample answers in this section.

- **Step 4**
  Reread the answering techniques in this section.

### Check your Time Management

● Suggested timing for this section:

- Paper 1, Section 1, Question B (50 marks): overall time allowance = **35 minutes** (includes planning time).

# Chapter 4

## Paper 1, Sec. II – Composing

This chapter contains the following items. You should tick the boxes as you complete each.

- Introduction ☐
- RPTA: Key Tips to Maximise Your Marks ☐
- Write a Talk or Speech ☐
- Write a Successful Narrative ☐
- Write a Personal Account ☐
- Write a Short Story ☐
- Key Exam Tips ☐
- Your Last Minute Revision! ☐

# Introduction

The Composing section is worth 100 marks. That means that up to 25 per cent of the marks for your entire Leaving Certificate English exam is awarded for your composition. It is crucial that you prepare well in advance for this question and not just leave it to luck on the day.

The Study Cards will help you to understand what is expected of you in the exam and remind you of the important techniques that can help you to earn top marks for your writing.

Read the sample compositions and take note of the techniques that make these answers effective. Practise using similar techniques in your own writing and use the Study Cards to check the key features of various composition styles.

## At a Glance

Section II, Composing includes seven titles and you are instructed to write a composition on any one. As you will discover from the 'Exam Trends' on page 117, questions on writing a talk, a speech, a narrative, a personal account, a newspaper or magazine article, and a short story have appeared frequently in this section of the exam paper.

Note also that the composition titles are intended to reflect your study of language in the areas of information, argument, persuasion, narration and the aesthetic use of language. In most compositions, these different types of language can mix and mingle. Just be aware of the type(s) of language you should use to make the best impression with the examiner.

### How Many Marks, How Much Time?

Section II Composing is worth **100 marks**.

Suggested time for planning and writing your answer is at least 1 hour: 15 minutes = 75 minutes.

## General Advice on Writing Your Composition

- When you have selected a composing title, you must then **brainstorm** for ideas and make a plan.

- You need to **plan** for your introduction (just a few opening lines is fine), followed by the main body of your composition. This should run to approximately two to three A4 pages and involve writing anything between six to 10 paragraphs. Finally, plan the key idea for your conclusion. Again, keep it concise; do not waffle or repeat everything you said before. Briefly summarise the key points of your talk or article or personal essay.

- Some students plan ideas in the form of a spider diagram or mind map. The main advantage of this type of plan is that you can see, at a glance, a 'picture' of your composition. It is easy to see how the ideas and paragraphs connect with one another. Also, it is very easy to add in new points at a later stage in your planning. Each leg of the 'spider' represents one paragraph. As you can see with the example on page 125, you simply jot down your ideas paragraph by paragraph, then delete any you think are not so strong. Develop the better ideas, discussing them, using examples, personal experiences, quotations and so on to illustrate your key point.

- Other students prefer to plan using a simple linear or table structure. Use bullets or numbered paragraphs and then jot down opposite each the key ideas for that paragraph.

- The advantages of this type of plan include it being very clear and easy to follow. It can be done quite quickly; just a few minutes and your plan can be in place. Sometimes, however, it may be hard to add in additional ideas without making the plan seem disorganised. Nonetheless, it is quick and simple and well worth trying out.

- Whichever type of plan you prefer, remember that planning is a must. Practise using both styles of plan and, in the exam, use the shape that suits you better.

- As with all writing, **keep your sentences clear and concise**. Do not rush your answer. You have adequate time to allow for planning, writing and checking over your work. Remain calm and relaxed and follow your plan through, step by step, working on one paragraph at a time.

- **Punctuate accurately** and observe the rules of grammar.

- **Keep your answer focused.** Check, while planning, that each paragraph is relevant to the title.

- Before you begin each paragraph, refer back to your plan to guide you. This will also help you to keep focused on the title.

- It is important to leave a few minutes at the end to **reread your answer** and to make any minor changes in expression or spelling.

- In terms of length, there is no right or wrong amount of words to write. Do not waste time counting words. In school and at home, **practise using the time available** to you (75 minutes), and use it to the full. If you can plan, write and check over three pages of A4 in 75 minutes, then that is what you should aim for in the exam. If you can manage four pages of A4, that is also fine.

- While quality is obviously important, do not write less than about two-and-a-half A4 pages, no matter how good it is! You need at least this length to develop your ideas and make your composition engaging and interesting. Remember, the question is worth 100 marks, so one or one-and-a-half A4 pages are just not enough.

## Exam Trends

### Recent Trends in Paper 1, Section II, Composing

| | 2001 | 2002 | 2003 | 2004 | 2005 | 2006 | 2007 | 2008 | 2009 | 2010 | 2011 | 2012 | 2013 |
|---|---|---|---|---|---|---|---|---|---|---|---|---|---|
| Write a talk or speech | ✓ | ✓ | ✓ | ✓ | ✓ | ✓ | ✓✓ | ✓ | ✓ | ✓ | ✓ | ✓ | ✓ |
| Write a personal essay – 'narrative' approach (emphasis on story) | ✓✓ | ✓✓ | ✓✓ | ✓✓ | ✓ | ✓ | ✓ | ✓ | ✓ | ✓ | ✓ | | |
| Write a personal essay – 'account' approach (emphasis on reflection) | ✓ | ✓✓ | ✓✓ | ✓ | ✓✓✓ | ✓✓ | ✓✓ | ✓✓ | ✓✓ | ✓ | ✓✓ | ✓✓ | ✓✓ |
| Write a short story | ✓ | ✓✓ | ✓ | ✓✓ | ✓✓ | ✓✓ | ✓✓ | ✓✓ | ✓✓ | ✓✓ | ✓ | ✓✓ | ✓✓ |
| Write an article for a magazine or newspaper | ✓✓ | | ✓ | ✓ | | ✓ | | ✓ | ✓ | ✓✓ | ✓ | ✓✓ | ✓✓ |
| Write a series of diary entries | | | | | | | | | | | ✓ | | |

## RPTA

### Key Tips to Maximise your Marks

RPTA:
Read
Plan
Time
Answer

### 🔑 Key Tip 1: READ the Question Correctly

● You can expect seven composing titles in this section. You only write a composition on any one of the titles. Take your time deciding which composition to write. Your decision here is really important. This question is worth 100 marks; that is 25 per cent of the total marks for your Leaving Certificate English exam.

Here is a useful tip from a student who sat her exam two years ago.

### Bright Spark – a Student's Tip

'When I read the seven titles on the exam paper, there were four that I knew that I would not do. Out of the other three, I had two favourites, but I could not choose which one to pick. I knew this was a really important decision. Then I remembered what our teacher suggested if we were stuck. I circled the two titles that I thought I could write best on. I wrote each title down into my answer booklet, and then for about 3 minutes, I brainstormed each title separately.

This gave me a brief plan of ideas for each of the two titles. Now when I looked at the two titles, I could clearly see which had the better ideas to work on. That was the title I chose. It was a good decision.

My advice to other students is, if you see a title that you really like, then go for it. If you are unsure about one or two titles, brainstorm as I did and when your ideas are on the page it should make that choice easier to make.'

*Sarah Jane*

● When you read your chosen title, there are three important things for you to work out:

### 1. What are you instructed to write?

If the question tells you to write a talk, do not write a speech for a debate. It is not the same thing. Similarly, a narrative is not the same as a personal essay. After studying this unit, you should become much clearer about what is actually expected of you.

> Make sure you know the difference between a talk and a formal speech, or between a personal narrative and a personal account.

### 2. Who are you writing for?

This is important because it helps you to plan both what you are going to write and how you are going to write it. For example, if you were asked to write a school magazine article for teenagers, then your language can be quite informal, chatty and relaxed. Writing in too formal a style for such an audience would be inappropriate. Your language register (vocabulary and tone) must be appropriate to your audience. If the audience is not specified, then you can take it that you are writing for a general readership or for an imagined audience of your own choosing.

### 3. Why are you writing?

In reading your title, be clear about the purpose of your writing, in other words, why you are writing. Are you writing a short story to entertain your audience, or perhaps a magazine article to inform your audience? Perhaps you are writing a speech to persuade your audience, or a narrative to share some personal experiences.

> Make sure that you answer the question asked.

Therefore, read your composing title at least three times, then underline or highlight the key terms in that title. Make sure you know what you are writing, who you are writing for, and why you are writing. This will help you to understand how to write your composition and which language categories to use most. When you are clear about the what, who, why and how, begin to work on your answer plan.

## Key Tip 2: PLAN Your Answer

● In planning what to write, make sure your points are relevant and appropriate.

● This question is awarded the highest amount of marks (100 out of 400 for both papers, or 25 per cent of the total exam), so you really must plan your composing answer in some detail. Some students brainstorm using a spider diagram. You will see some examples below. Other students prefer to plan their ideas into a simple linear plan. Experiment with different types of plan until you find one that is right for you.

● Another reason to plan is that a longer answer will be expected for 100 marks: two-and-a-half to four A4 pages. You do not want to run out of ideas after one A4 page. Unfortunately, it happens to students every year. So, plan before you begin writing your composition. If, after 5 minutes of planning, you are stuck and can only think of one or two ideas, then perhaps this is not the title for you. Consider a different title.

**119**

**HINT**

Each composition title is linked with one text. You may refer to, quote from or use any ideas (for characters, setting, issues, and so on) from each of the three comprehending texts if you wish. But do not copy out large chunks of description.

Short compositions will not be awarded high marks! In your plan, make sure your points are interesting and relevant to the title. Also, your plan must have sufficient points that when developed will cover two-and-a-half to four A4 pages.

### Key Tip 3: TIME Your Answer

Time Allowed (Paper 1):
2 Hours 50 Minutes

- The total time allowed for Paper 1 is 2 hours, 50 minutes (170 minutes).

### Suggested Time for this Section

**Section II Composing (100 Marks)**

Suggested Time:
1 Hours 15 Minutes

- This includes planning time and time to read over your composition to check for accuracy in layout, paragraphing, spelling and grammar.

### Key Tip 4: ANSWER the Question Asked

- Just before you begin to write your full answer, look once again at your selected title, then at your plan. If you think your plan is not directly answering **each** key term or instruction in the title, you have time to make slight changes now.

- **CHECKLIST**

  - Make sure you are writing what you were asked to write, for example, a personal essay, or talk, or newspaper article.

  - Make sure you are aware of your audience. Your content and language must be appropriate to this audience.

  - Make sure you know why you are writing.

  - Check again your time allowance for the question, then begin.

# Write a Talk or Speech

## ◉ What Kind of Titles to Expect

Here are some of the titles on writing a talk or speech under Section II, Composing from past exam papers. Each composition is worth **100 marks**.

> Revise the notes on writing a talk or speech on page 78

- **In Text 1, Des Bishop tells us that his mother was the boss in his family when he and his brothers were growing up.**
  Write a speech in which you are for or against the motion: that rules and regulations are important in life. (LC, OL, 2013)

- **'. . .our global Irish family nurtures a deep loyalty to Irish identify and culture.'**
  Write a speech, to be delivered to your year group, in which you express your views on the importance of Irish cultural pursuits such as music, sport, drama etc. (LC, OL, 2012)

- **'. . .a new vision that as human beings we could do better.'**
  Write a talk you would give at your school graduation ceremony encouraging your classmates to play their full part as citizens of Ireland and the world. (LC, OL, 2011)

- **'. . .and finishing it gave me a great sense of achievement.'**
  Write a talk about a person/people whose achievements you admire. (LC, OL, 2010)

- **'I couldn't wait for the rest of the 1960s to begin.'**
  Write a talk you would give to your classmates about what you imagine life will be like in the year 2060. (LC, OL, 2009)

- **'Grab life with both hands.'**
  Write the speech you would give to a group of young people on the importance of having a positive attitude towards life. (LC, OL, 2008)

- **'. . .his lonely march for survival.'**
  Write a speech for a debate in which you argue for or against the motion: that people should not take unnecessary risks. (LC, OL, 2007)

- **'We also spoke to a group of parents.'**
  Write out the talk you would give to parents about your experience of being a teenager. (LC, OL, 2006)

- **'. . .every moment seemed important to me. . .'**
  Write a speech you would give to a group of young people on the things that you think are important in life. (LC, OL, 2005)

## Study Card No.18: How to Write a Successful Talk or Speech

- A talk, a speech to a group of people, and a speech for a debate are similar in many ways. You have to prepare points on a topic and write them out so that they are clear, coherent and interesting to your audience.

- However, writing a speech can be a little different to writing a talk. Here are a few tips that apply to writing a more formal speech that might be helpful.

- If the speech is for a group of young people, you may simply introduce yourself, say why you are here and briefly indicate what you are going to speak about: *'Good morning everyone/students, my name is Gerard Thomas and I'm very happy to be here to speak to you today about the importance of having a positive attitude towards life.'*

- This kind of speech is slightly more formal than a talk. The subject is often more general or universal. A talk is often on a more personal subject. For example, previous titles have included:

  - *Write out a talk that you would give to a group of young people telling them how to look good and feel good about themselves.* (LC, OL, 2003)

  - *Write out the talk you would give to parents about your experience of being a teenager.* (LC, OL, 2006)

- Compare this with:

  - *Write the speech that you would give to a group of your classmates about things you would change in the world.* (LC, OL, 2002)

  - *Write a speech for a debate in which you argue for or against the motion: 'that people should not take unnecessary risks'.* (LC, OL, 2007)

- The subject of a talk tends to be more conversational, the language more chatty and relaxed. You can use colloquialisms, abbreviations, even slang in a talk, which might be out of place in a speech.

- Even more formal is a speech written for a debate. The opening to a debate speech often begins with a formal introduction, e.g. 'Chairperson, adjudicators, members of the opposition [or 'proposition' if you are going to oppose the motion], ladies and gentlemen, fellow students, I am here today to propose the motion that "The future is bleak".' (LC, OL, 2001)

- You can introduce briefly the key areas you are about to discuss: 'In my speech today I want to discuss three aspects of the motion': 'First', 'Secondly', and finally, 'I will'.

- You then take each point in turn and develop it in one paragraph.
- As with a talk, you can make your speech persuasive by using facts, personal anecdotes and quotations to support your points.
- You can also use emotive language – try to connect with your listener's hearts and minds.
- Why not include a short anecdote (personal experience) to make a key point memorable.
- You might also anticipate what the other side might say and then tell your audience why those points are incorrect.
- At the end of your speech, briefly summarise the key points that you made. Begin as follows: 'Ladies and gentlemen, I am sure you can see clearly that', 'I have proven to you that', 'I have shown you that'. In your closing line, you might finish as follows: 'I am Greg Norman and I beg to propose the motion'.
- Do not worry too much if you forget how to use the formal beginning and closing of a debate speech. The points that you make in the main body of your speech are far more important.

## From the Exam Papers

Read the composing title below from the 2008 paper. Underline or highlight the key terms of the title. Work out *what* you have to write, *who* you are writing for, and *why* you are writing. These three factors will help you to decide *how* to write your speech.

Make a plan and then write your speech. Compare your answer with the sample speech below.

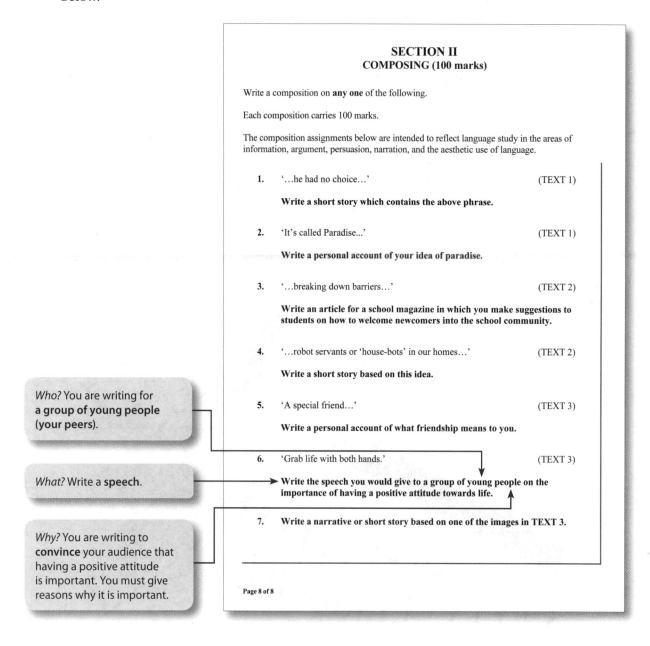

**SECTION II**
**COMPOSING (100 marks)**

Write a composition on **any one** of the following.

Each composition carries 100 marks.

The composition assignments below are intended to reflect language study in the areas of information, argument, persuasion, narration, and the aesthetic use of language.

1. '…he had no choice…' (TEXT 1)

   **Write a short story which contains the above phrase.**

2. 'It's called Paradise...' (TEXT 1)

   **Write a personal account of your idea of paradise.**

3. '…breaking down barriers…' (TEXT 2)

   **Write an article for a school magazine in which you make suggestions to students on how to welcome newcomers into the school community.**

4. '…robot servants or 'house-bots' in our homes…' (TEXT 2)

   **Write a short story based on this idea.**

5. 'A special friend…' (TEXT 3)

   **Write a personal account of what friendship means to you.**

6. 'Grab life with both hands.' (TEXT 3)

   **Write the speech you would give to a group of young people on the importance of having a positive attitude towards life.**

7. **Write a narrative or short story based on one of the images in TEXT 3.**

Page 8 of 8

*Who?* You are writing for **a group of young people (your peers).**

*What?* Write a **speech**.

*Why?* You are writing to **convince** your audience that having a positive attitude is important. You must give reasons why it is important.

## ◉ Student's Answer Plan

### Linear Plan Shape

- Introduction – greet audience, introduce myself, and say why I'm here.
- Paragraph 2 – share personal thoughts on topic with audience – why ask me?
- Paragraph 3 – how a positive attitude has helped me.
- Paragraph 4 – examples of sporting heroes – they have a positive attitude.
- Paragraph 5 – my TY experience – Zambia – the children there.
- Paragraph 6 – famous people with positive attitude, e.g. JFK, Mandela.
- Paragraph 7 – drive home key points about importance of positive attitude.
- Conclusion – finish with thanks and an appropriate quote.

**Note on language:** Use narrative and persuasive language. Some information and argument also. Perhaps one or two aesthetic images.

### Spider Diagram Plan

You can see above that this student has used a simple, yet effective, linear plan. The very same points in a spider diagram (spidergram) might look like this:

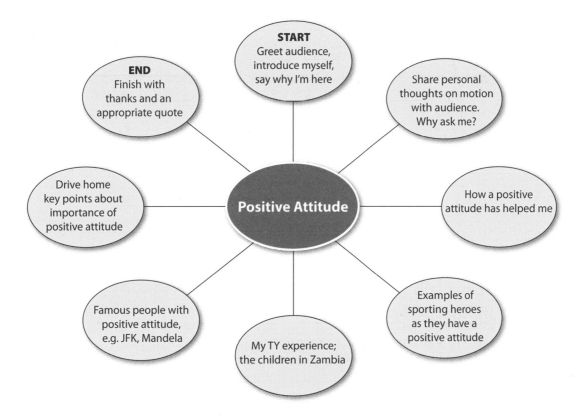

## Sample Speech

### The Importance of Having a Positive Attitude in Life

Good morning students.

Some of you probably know me: my name is Jennifer Corrigan and I'm a sixth-year student here in the school. Your Year Head, Ms Deasy, asked me if I'd speak to you today, just briefly, on the importance of having a positive attitude in life.

I have to admit, when Ms Deasy approached me last week and asked if I would like to speak in Assembly, I was bit terrified at the idea. And then when she told me I'd have to speak about the importance of having a positive attitude, I nearly died! My first reaction was 'why me?' I mean, our school team as you know, lost the girls Gaelic football final last year, and I was the losing captain. Later in the year, I missed out on a chance to play for my county when I fractured a bone in my ankle in training. And what is even worse, I scored 180 points in my mock results this year and I'm hoping to study engineering in college! So you can probably understand why I was asking myself, why me?

But then it dawned on me, perhaps I am the right person to speak to you about having a positive attitude. You see, one thing I have discovered over the past year, is that to be positive in your attitude does not mean that you are successful in everything you do. Being positive, I know now, means being able to drive towards your dreams, and if you reach them well and good. But if you do not, that is where a positive attitude is even more important. I did not take defeat lying down. OK, I was devastated when we lost the county final last year, but two months later, I was back training in the cold winter nights, fighting to keep my place on the school team. I discovered that winning is important to me, but participating, and giving my best is even more important.

However, this does not mean that a positive attitude in life will not bring success. On the contrary, a positive attitude is one of the key ingredients in achieving success. In the sporting arena, would individuals such as Shay Given, Padraig Harrington, or Brian O'Driscoll have enjoyed such success without a positive attitude? I am sure, that most of these successful individuals tasted failure in their early careers. But failure for these great heroes was only another stepping stone towards success. Just imagine, we might never have heard of them or enjoyed their success if they had not used a positive attitude to lift themselves up and begin again with even more determination. The legendary boxer Muhammad Ali once said, 'To be a great champion you must believe you are the best. If you're not, pretend you are'. So you see, I do not think having a positive attitude is always about being the best, it is about giving your best.

Some of you may decide to enter TY next year. I studied TY two years ago and it was one of the best years in school for me. You'll remember that our school sent 10 students over to Zambia to work with the children of a small village school for two weeks. I was lucky enough to have been chosen. Can I tell you that if ever you need proof of the power and importance of a positive attitude, then look to places like Zambia. There, the children had it in bucketfuls! They had little money, few personal possessions, no mobile phones, no after school musicals or battle of the bands, no Twitter, no blogs, no iTunes, but they certainly had an abundance of positive attitude. The spirit of these people taught me that you must never give up. I brought food and money to help them, but they gave me something far more important – hope.

Indeed, a positive attitude and hope go hand in hand. Over time there are many great examples of people who never let go of their belief in a better way. Think of John F. Kennedy, Martin Luther King, and Nelson Mandela. Closer to home, think of the Irish politicians who fought long and hard for the Good Friday Agreement in 1998 that eventually brought peace to our own island. The many great achievements of these people, too numerous to mention, would not have been possible without a positive attitude. And their positive attitude brought hope and belief, pride and peace into the hearts of millions of people all over the world.

Students, I have sat on those chairs where you sit now. I know how important your Third Year in school is for you. I hope I have been able to show you that having a positive attitude is extremely important, not just in school, but in life in general. Being positive keeps you going, not always to be first but to give of your best. Having a positive attitude has helped me to go for my dreams, to believe in myself again, to know I can do it and that once I give it my best I will never fail. Negativity is draining. It makes you cynical about the world and even about yourself. It does not bring out the best in those around you. A positive attitude on the other hand is a bright light in a sea fog. It lifts the gloom and shows a better way. It shouts out I can do it, when others think perhaps that you cannot.

An American writer, Emily Dickinson, once compared hope to a small bird that 'sings the tune without the words and never stops at all'. She believed in the power of hope, in the importance of having a positive attitude towards life. I still believe I can study engineering in college. That is my dream. I hope you will always believe in your dreams too.

Thank you for your attention.

## Answering Techniques

- **Greet the target audience** in an appropriate way. Introduce yourself and explain why you are here.

- Use narrative language to introduce the speech – note the **personal anecdote**. It is a good way to grab the attention and interest of your audience.

- The paragraph opens with a **topic sentence**; this states the key point and is developed through the rest of the paragraph.

- The audience is the speaker's own peers who would find it easy to identify with the **personal story** of the speaker.

- Note the use of **linking phrases or connectives**, these make the speech more coherent and easier to follow, e.g. 'Indeed…'.

- Other linking phrases you could use to add to a key point include: 'Furthermore', 'In addition', 'Not only that but'.

- **Rhetorical questions** involve the audience and win their agreement.

- Well-known figures from the world of sport are used as examples to support key points.

- The discussion is broadened out. Other examples of people with a positive approach to life are introduced.

- Speaker gives real examples of real children with a positive attitude.

- Address your audience in a warm, personal way. Draw them into the speech. Let them know that you understand their position, where they stand in life.

- Note the use of **aesthetic language**: the metaphor of the bright light should be memorable long after the speech has concluded.

- **Finish on an uplifting and positive note.** Use quotations. Return to the opening ideas of the speech (college) to give a sense of completeness. Wish your audience well and thank the students for their attention.

# Write a Successful Narrative

## What Kind of Titles to Expect

Here are some of the titles on writing a narrative from past exam papers. Each composition is worth **100 marks**.

- **'I recalled just how wonderful my life had been to get me to this point.'**
  Write about a time in your life when you achieved something that really mattered to you. (LC, OL, 2011)

- **'The toughest event in the world.'**
  Write about a time in your life when you took part in a demanding event. (LC, OL, 2010)

- **'We were in the right place at the right time.'**
  Write about a time when you found yourself in the right place at the right time. (LC, OL, 2009)

- Write a narrative or short story based on one of the images in Text 3. (LC, OL, 2008)

- **'. . .the bravest decision of his life. . .'**
  Tell about a time in your life when you had a difficult choice to make. (LC, OL, 2007)

- **'When I was small.'**
  Tell about some of your best and worst experiences of being a young child. (LC, OL, 2006)

- **'Suddenly the evening changed. . .'**
  Write about a time when you experienced change in your life. (LC, OL, 2006)

- Write a story based on any one of the images in Text 3. (LC, OL, 2005)

- **'Every head was out of the carriage windows to stare at our embarrassment.'**
  Write about a time when you felt embarrassed. (LC, OL, 2005)

## Study Card No.19: How to Write a Successful Narrative

- In a narrative, you focus on telling a story.

- Many of the narrative titles ask for a personal story: 'Write about a time in your life', 'Write about a time when you felt embarrassed', 'Tell about a time when one of your dreams came true.'

- A personal narrative has a simple structure – usually a straightforward beginning, middle and end. It must be written from your viewpoint, so use 'I' frequently as you tell the story.

- The characters in your story may be real or imaginary.

- There is no need to explore any theme in great depth in a simple narrative.

- Nonetheless, you must make your narrative/story interesting. Use descriptive language to paint clear word-pictures of people and their actions and the places that they move around in.

- A personal narrative may be based on your own real life experiences. This type of narrative is loosely autobiographical. Such stories are usually very interesting and have real conviction behind them. The readers sense that they are getting a glimpse of a real and significant moment in a person's life. Such an approach would be perfect for questions such as:

  - *Tell about a time when one of your dreams came true* (LC, OL, 2003).

- However, you may make up the whole thing if you wish! But, do not announce that in your story. Write it as if it really did happen to you. Your story must have an air of reality about it. If it sounds autobiographical, it is usually more interesting for the examiner to read.

- Sometimes a fictitious/imaginary narrative might be more suitable. This approach would suit narratives similar to:

  - *'This is my life...' Imagine you are in the world of one of the pictures in Text 3. Tell your story.* (LC, OL, 2001)

- Whether your story is real or imaginary, you must use a first-person narrator. 'I' did this and 'I' did that is what is needed here. The examiner wants to know what happened to *you* in particular, how *you* reacted, behaved or felt.

- In both real and imaginary narratives, the focus of your narrative should be on describing the situation or event where you felt threatened, happy or proud. The question will instruct you and give your writing a focus.

- You may take a serious or humorous approach. Writing a humorous narrative can be quite difficult, so if you have not been practising this in school, it would be best not to try writing your first humorous narrative in your actual exam!

- Remember, as a narrator, you may comment on the events in your narrative, but keep the focus on the 'telling' of the story.

## From the Exam Papers

Read the composing title below from the 2006 paper. Underline or highlight the key terms of the title. Work out *what* you have to write, *who* you are writing for, and *why* you are writing. These three factors will help you to decide *how* to write your narrative.

Make a plan and then write your personal narrative. Compare your answer with the sample narrative below.

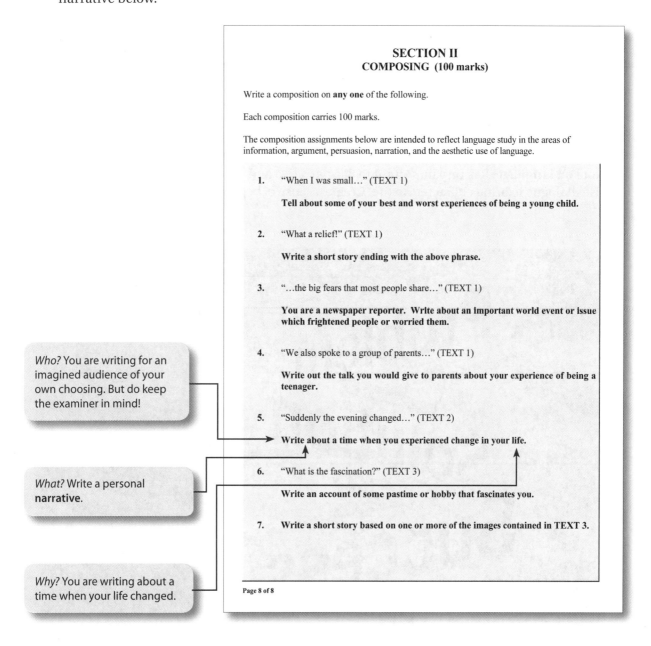

**SECTION II**
**COMPOSING (100 marks)**

Write a composition on **any one** of the following.

Each composition carries 100 marks.

The composition assignments below are intended to reflect language study in the areas of information, argument, persuasion, narration, and the aesthetic use of language.

1.  "When I was small…" (TEXT 1)

    **Tell about some of your best and worst experiences of being a young child.**

2.  "What a relief!" (TEXT 1)

    **Write a short story ending with the above phrase.**

3.  "…the big fears that most people share…" (TEXT 1)

    **You are a newspaper reporter. Write about an important world event or issue which frightened people or worried them.**

4.  "We also spoke to a group of parents…" (TEXT 1)

    **Write out the talk you would give to parents about your experience of being a teenager.**

5.  "Suddenly the evening changed…" (TEXT 2)

    **Write about a time when you experienced change in your life.**

6.  "What is the fascination?" (TEXT 3)

    **Write an account of some pastime or hobby that fascinates you.**

7.  **Write a short story based on one or more of the images contained in TEXT 3.**

Page 8 of 8

*Who?* You are writing for an imagined audience of your own choosing. But do keep the examiner in mind!

*What?* Write a personal **narrative**.

*Why?* You are writing about a time when your life changed.

## ◉ Student's Answer Plan

**Beginning**

- Tuesday 18 September – an important day; make reader curious.
- Maths teacher – use dialogue to create tense atmosphere and conflict.
- Room 7 – first meeting with Julie Bell; the big moment.

**Middle**

- Tell how our relationship developed over time – Facebook.
- Fear of failure with mock exams.
- Julie's help made a difference.

**End**

- Kavanagh sees improvement.
- Opening exam result – changed me, more self-belief and a new friend.

**Note on language:** It is very important to use narrative and descriptive language. Use dialogue to bring characters to life. Create a sense of beginning, middle and end.

## Sample Narrative Answer

**To 'B' or not to 'B'**

I will never forget the day. Tuesday, 18 September 2007. It was the first time I heard the name Julie Bell, the first time I saw those beautiful blue eyes, the first time I admitted to myself that something had to change.

'Burns! Where's your homework today then?'
'Don't know Sir'.

'Don't know. And, eh, would you have actually done it at all Burns?'

'I think I did, Sir, I'm not sure.'
'Right, detention, 1 o'clock Room 7,' boomed Kavanagh as the rest of the class jeered and laughed – again.

This was the third time since returning to school that old Kavers had given me detention. I mean nobody else in the class does homework for him either, but I always get the chop.

'But Sir, I can't do those maths . . .'
'Won't do, is more like it Burns,' sneered Mr Kavanagh, 'that's enough out of you for today, 1 o'clock. Sharp.'

Now I don't mean to be unfair to Kavers, but I really think he had reached his 'best before date' and retirement was beckoning. So he seemed to want to vent his years of pent-up anger and stress at me! I don't know what I ever did to him. Okay, I did find maths difficult, I always did. But, it was no use trying to explain that to Sir, his reply was always the same: 'Room 7, 1 o'clock. Sharp.'

I swallowed the last bite of my cheese sandwich with my pride and opened the red door. I expected to see the usual suspects inside: Brady from Year 2, Swan from Year 1 and Kelly and Rogers from Year 5. I was the only Third Year victim. But was I? Sitting behind the top desk right in front of Kavers was a new face. It hardly noticed my meek arrival at detention.

'Sit down Burns, you're one minute late. No, sit here'. Kavers put me sitting right next to the new girl. She didn't even blink.
'Your work is on the board.'
Just then, the secretary came over the intercom: 'Would Mr Kavanagh come to the office for an urgent message please.' Kavers left immediately.

Kelly and Rogers skipped through the door shortly after Kavers, not bothering to wait to see if he'd return.

Five minutes later and I was alone with her. Finally, she glanced over at me, with the most amazing blue eyes.

'Hi'. That was it. I was hooked. Just that one syllable, more powerful, more meaningful than all the words of every play, every poem ever written by William Shakespeare. She said, 'Hi'. And believe it or not, that was the moment that changed my life for ever. That was Julie Bell on 18 September 2007, at 1.05p.m. in Room 7. Let me explain.

Three months after we first spoke, Julie and I were still the best of friends. We did the usual things together, exchanged mobile numbers, hung out after school and over the weekends, you know, the usual stuff. Within the first few weeks, we were chatting online for hours, sharing stories from the classroom and gossip from the corridors. We became the best of virtual friends too, on Facebook. But it was in the real world, following those weeks and months when we first met, that we grew closer and began to trust one another, dare I say love one another more. Julie was just magical – and bright too, straight As in her Christmas exams.

Coming up to my Junior Cert mocks in February, I really started to panic. I had so much work to do and so little time. History would be fine, and Geography OK. English shouldn't be too bad, and French easy enough. Science would be a nightmare, but Maths, now Maths would be a disaster. Julie could see I was stressing over the exams.

'Don't worry about the mocks, just do your best,' was her usual advice.
'But I'm going to fail, I just know I am.'
'Fail what?,' she asked, turning towards me in the canteen one afternoon.
'Well, maths for starters.'
'Maths?'
'Yeah, maths. Don't you remember, that first day in Room 7, with Kavers...'
''Course I remember, but . . .'
'Well, I was there because, well, I'm just useless at maths.'
'You can't be, you're . . .'
'It's OK for you to say Julie, you're in the Higher Level class, but I'm struggling, I'm hopeless, even at Ordinary Level.'

It may sound silly, juvenile even, but I felt as if I'd revealed a long, dark secret to Julie. It was almost a relief that she finally knew, I was going to flunk maths. I felt embarrassed, felt a failure.

Julie stood up, firmly, pointed her finger at me and spoke in a slow, determined voice.

'Michael Burns, I can guarantee you, that you will not fail your maths exam in the Junior Cert.'

How do you follow that? All I could do was chuckle. But Julie wasn't joking. She meant it and not only that, she proved it.

Every Friday evening Julie went through the chapters Kavers had whizzed through during the week. She was patient and really helpful. She explained things slowly and clearly, then asked me to try some examples. I went along with it all for the first few weeks. I mean, my parents were happy and I was happy, just to spend more time with Julie. But soon I realised that I was actually improving. And I just knew I could do it one Monday morning when Kavers stood up and announced to the class: 'Good work Burns, I can see you've decided to do some work at last. You might just pass Maths yet, lad, you just might.'

So today, it's almost a year later. Five minutes ago, I was handed a brown envelope by our Principal, Mrs James. I walked calmly out of the building to meet Julie at the basketball courts. I opened the envelope, unfolded my results and there it was in black and white, Mathematics, Gnáthleibhéal B. I had achieved what I never thought possible. It was one of the proudest moments of my short life. And when I look back now, I just know that Tuesday, 18 September 2007, at 1.05p.m. was the moment that made it happen. From that day on, my time in Third Year brought an important change in my life: I made a great new friend in Julie Bell, and I began to believe that no matter how difficult a task may seem, with hard work, good advice and clear guidance, I can do it! Even old Kavers would be proud!

## Answering Techniques

- **Set the context of the narrative** – an important day – leave the reader in suspense.

- **Introduce characters**: keep it to one or two. Use dialogue to add realism and create an impression of the characters.

- Use a first-person narrator. You are the 'I' in the story; the narrative is told from your point of view.

- Remember to use paragraphs. Many paragraphs in a narrative can be quite short, e.g. three or four lines.

- Note that **the transition** to the middle section of the narrative – 'Three months after we first spoke' – is done very quickly. There is no need to go into tedious detail about every day/week spent together.

- Show how the relationship developed.

- The plot is kept simple – this is not a short story; keep the focus on the difficulty with maths.

- As narrator, you can break from your descriptions to make some brief comments on the characters or the events.

- The narrative has moved on towards the end section. Again, note how the transition is made very simply: 'So today, it's almost a year later.'

- Keep the focus of your ending very much on the title of the composition: 'A time when you experienced change in your life'. **Reflect on the title** and on what has changed about you because of the experiences in your story.

# Write a Personal Account

## What Kind of Titles to Expect

Here are some of the titles on writing a personal essay/account from past exam papers. Each composition is worth 100 marks.

- **In Text 2, Gary Larson believes that drawing is a continuous learning process.**
  Write a personal essay in which you consider the important lessons you have learned in life. (LC, OL, 2013)

- **In Text 3, Michael McIntyre tells us that he had his own point of view and outlook on life.**
  Write a personal essay about your views on ONE of the following topics: – music – money – happiness. (LC, OL, 2013)

- **'. . . the celebrity status that comes with twenty-first century fame.'**
  Write a personal essay about your views on celebrities and being famous in the twenty-first century. (LC, OL, 2012)

- **'...I was completely ignored...'**
  Write a personal account of an occasion when you felt you were being ignored. (LC, OL, 2011)

- **'At times like that you make friends very easily.'**
  Write a personal account of the challenges of making and keeping friends. (LC, OL, 2010)

- **'New Year's Eve . . . A light snowfall.'**
  Write a personal account of your favourite memories of Christmas and the New Year. (LC, OL, 2009)

- **'The toughest event in the world.'**
  Write about a time in your life when you took part in a demanding event. (LC, OL, 2008)

- **'A special friend.'**
  Write a personal account of what friendship means to you. (LC, OL, 2008)

- **'The many faces of success.'**
  Write a personal account of what success means to you. (LC, OL, 2007)

- **'What is the fascination?'**
  Write an account of some pastime or hobby that fascinates you. (LC, OL, 2006)

- **'What freedom means to me. . .'**
  Write a personal account of what freedom means to you. (LC, OL, 2005)

## Study Card No.20: How to Write a Successful Personal Account

- A personal account and a narrative are both types of personal essay.
- A personal essay that discusses a topic is a personal account.
- A personal essay that tells a story is a personal narrative.

- A personal account is not quite the same as a personal narrative. Narrative essays usually ask you to tell a story or write about a time when you did this or that, tell about a time when you felt proud, etc. The focus in a narrative is on the story.

- A personal account is a little different. This composition asks you to reflect on and give your opinions on a particular topic. The discussion element of the personal account is very important.

- For example, in a personal account, you may describe situations and events which you yourself were involved in (loosely autobiographical). The focus, however, must be on describing and reflecting on your own personal attitudes and feelings on a particular topic.

- Study the composition titles, looking for a personal account. They may ask for your ideas, e.g. 'Write a personal account of your idea of paradise' (2008). They may ask for your opinion on issues, e.g. 'Write a personal account of what friendship means to you' (2008). They may ask something like 'Write a personal account of what home means to you' (2004). You can see from these titles, they are really looking for a discussion not a narrative The focus is on your opinions and reflections, not your story.

- Nonetheless, if your personal experiences can support and illustrate your opinions, include these too.

- The tone in a personal account should be intimate as you are sharing personal thoughts with your audience; you are, in a way, letting them enter into a small part of your world. Your own personality should come through in your writing.

- You know now that in a personal account you are expected to pass comment on issues, events, experiences, or situations. You should explore what you learned from them, how they informed you, shocked you, delighted you or surprised you and so on. This is what gives a sense of reflection to a personal account.

- You may use a brief anecdote as a springboard from which to explore your point of view.

- You may also use or refer to ideas in any of the three texts on the exam paper.

- You should use clear, descriptive writing. Informative and persuasive language is also important in a personal account.

- Finally, use the personal pronoun 'I' throughout the essay.

## From the Exam Papers

Read the composing title below from the 2010 paper. Underline or highlight the key terms of the title. Work out *what* you have to write, *who* you are writing for, and *why* you are writing. These three factors will help you to decide *how* to write your personal account.

Make a plan and then write your personal account. Compare your answer with the sample personal account below.

---

### SECTION II
### COMPOSING (100 marks)

Write a composition on **any one** of the following.

Each composition carries 100 marks.

The composition assignments below are intended to reflect language study in the areas of information, argument, persuasion, narration, and the aesthetic use of language.

1. '… and finishing it gave me a great sense of achievement.' (Text 1)

   **Write a talk about a person/people whose achievements you admire.**

2. 'The toughest event in the world.' (Text 1)

   **Write about a time in your life when you took part in a demanding event.**

3. 'At times like that you make friends very easily.' (Text 1)

   **Write a personal account of the challenges of making and keeping friends.**

4. 'Night came. A dirty, black night with rain.' (Text 2)

   **Write a short story based on the above phrase.**

5. 'There was another small tent, not much bigger than a good-sized kennel.' (Text 2)

   **Write a humorous article about camping.**

6. 'Ignoring the Restricted Area sign I just kept walking …' (Text 3)

   **Write a short story inspired by the above phrase.**

7. Look at the images in Text 3. (Text 3)

   **Write an article for a teenage magazine for or against the use of animals in sport.**

Page 8 of 12

---

*Who?* You are writing for a general audience.

*What?* Write a personal account.

*Why?* You are writing to express your opinions on the challenges of making and keeping friends.

## ◉ Student's Answer Plan

**Challenges of making and keeping friends:**

**Introduction**

● Seemed so easy, so natural in primary school.

● As I got older, harder to find real friends.

● As a teen, opportunities for making friends increased.

● Online 'friendships'.

● The importance of 'image'.

● Honesty and trust build real friendships.

**Conclusion**

● My own loyal friend.

## ◉ Sample Personal Account

I suppose I never really thought much about it until I was 13 or 14. You see, in primary school, making friends and keeping them seemed to come naturally. There was never much to it really. You bonded with the lads on your team, or with a few of the boys in your class. You played with your near neighbours on the green from the time you could walk. It all just seemed to happen. It was as natural as the leaves budding and falling each year from the trees we swung out of as kids. It was as if there was some invisible glue that very simply, yet very effectively, bonded you to a close set of friends. And that bond lasted for years.

I slowly began to realise that in life, making and keeping friends is not so simple. I suppose the first hunch I got that all was not well happened around Christmas of my First Year in secondary school. When every one else in my tutor group seemed to be giving and getting cards, I actually did not receive any at all, not one. Most of my friends from primary had moved on to other friends, something which surprised me. Don't get me wrong, I am totally in favour of making new friends but I also think keeping 'old' friends is just as important.

But things have moved on since then. As I grew into my teens I found that my social activities widened and I enjoyed many more situations where I could meet new friends. Weekend discos, house parties, the local soccer and Gaelic clubs, these all became key ways in which to meet new people. During the summer holidays I enrolled in a soccer school in Galway and there I met some great new pals. I found that, once you are open to making new friends it sometimes is not very difficult at all. In fact, sometimes the less you try, the easier it is! People with similar hobbies and pastimes seem to gel quite easily. Of course, some of these you never hear from again, but I am still in regular contact with three great friends I met in Galway.

Online, it has become easier than ever to meet new faces. I am not so sure I can call these people 'friends' but I do chat to them every week and we share personal information about our lives, what we do, where we go to enjoy ourselves, our likes and dislikes and so on. Virtual friends are fine, to a point. However, I will never forget one Friday evening calling around to my friend Jamie's house, to see if he wanted to hang out for an hour in the town. 'No, Jamie's too busy,' smiled his mother at the door, 'he is chatting with his online friends'. Believe me when I tell you, being replaced by a virtual friend is not a pleasant experience.

Of course, image seems to be everything nowadays. I sometimes think that if you are not sporting the latest gear, the coolest sweater, the meanest runners, the newest football jersey, the hottest phone, you are less of a person. Everyone wants to be around the 'in' crowd. And that is not just teens! We all have higher expectations of everything today. We want better schools, faster cars, bigger houses, more exotic holidays, and as for friends, well it seems they have to be from the top shelf too. But I am not convinced. I still think that the basic values of honesty and loyalty are crucially important to a real friendship, one that will stand the test of time.

I am not trying to suggest that I have tasted the salmon of knowledge here and know everything about making and keeping friends! But, I suppose many of my experiences have taught me that making new friends is not an automatic process and keeping them can sometimes be hard work. Friends for keeping are special people indeed. Such friendships should be cherished and not taken for granted. While I may have 30 'friends', I really have about 10 people I could call real friends. And my mum and dad are included. These are people who have made a difference in my life, and filled it with laughter and love, with support and advice when I needed it most.

But let me tell you briefly about one of the best and most loyal friends I have. Diarmuid Gaffney was six when I first met him in First Class primary. We have always been in the same class together, sharing pencils and crayons, even lunches. In secondary school, we both continued our friendship. What made us great friends was our shared interest in sport, our love of music and our desire to 'have a laugh'. We have come to trust one another and respect one another completely.

Making and keeping friends, special friends, is indeed challenging. But despite all the odds, it can be done. I am living proof of that.

## Answering Techniques

- Using the pronoun 'I' is very important as this is a personal account.

- **Aesthetic language can be used** sparingly – do not overdo it.

- Begin with a simple point, but do not get bogged down in big arguments at this stage in the essay.

- Remember, a personal account is not a narrative. Do not stay in story mode for too long. Break from the memory and **discuss your opinions and feelings**.

- Note how the writer mixes informative, narrative and persuasive language in paragraph 4.

- A new point is introduced in paragraph 5: the importance of image.

- The tone is warm and intimate without being condescending. Note how the writer balances knowledge with humility.

- Note also the **autobiographical flavour** of the account throughout.

- Return to the title of the composition in the conclusion. Make a final comment in line with the key points in your essay.

# Write a Short Story

## ◎ What Kind of Titles to Expect

Here are some of the titles on writing a short story from past exam papers.
Each composition is worth **100 marks**.

- **In Text 1, Des Bishop explains how his opinion of his father changed over time.**
  Write a short story in which one character's opinion of another character changes dramatically. (LC, OL, 2013)

- **In Text 2, Gary Larson writes about his fondness for wildlife.**
  Write a short story in which an animal or animals play an important part. (LC, OL, 2013)

- **'. . .to tackle giants. . .'**
  Write a short story inspired by the phrase, '. . .to tackle giants'. (LC, OL, 2012)

- **'. . . e-mail. . .mobile phone. . .browser. . .'**
  Write a short story in which modern technology plays an important part. (LC, OL, 2012)

- **'...in the future, life would be different'**
  Write a short story set in the future. (LC, OL, 2011)

- **'Night came. A dirty, black night with rain.'**
  Write a short story based on the above phrase. (LC, OL, 2010)

- **'Connections with foreign places.' (Text 3)**
  Write a narrative or short story inspired by image 3. (LC, OL, 2009)

- Write a narrative or short story based on one of the images in Text 3. (LC, OL, 2008)

- **'No one had heard of me. . .'**
  Write a short story which begins with the above phrase. (LC, OL, 2007)

- **'What a relief!'**
  Write a short story ending with the above phrase. (LC, OL, 2006)

- **'For God's sake do something. . .'**
  Write a short story beginning with the above phrase. (LC, OL, 2005)

## Study Card No.21: How to Write a Successful Short Story

- In your short story, there a few things you must do:

  - Create a clear beginning, middle and end in your story.

  - Create one (maximum two) central character(s).

  - Keep your story believable – your character does not have to save the world!

  - Create some sense of tension and conflict leading up to a climax.

  - The climax should be the central part of your story – it is a crucial or key moment for your characters. It usually comes in the middle or near the end of a story.

  - Issues, problems, in the story should be sorted out in some way in your ending (resolution).

● Planning

- A good plan should include ideas on each of the following essential features of a short story:

**SETTING**

- You have to decide on a time and place in which your story's action occurs. Use vivid, clear language to create an interesting place. Describe sights, smells, sounds, anything that helps to **make the place seem real** for your reader. Do not try to describe everything about the place, just a few important details. In terms of time, your story might be set in the past, present or future. Most stories are set in the past and told in the past tense. The events in the story should occur over a short time span – perhaps a few hours, or a day. Generally, avoid stories that span weeks or months.

- Many students prepare a description of a setting before the exam. This is fine, but remember, you may have to adapt it a little (or a lot) in the exam to keep it relevant to the title.

**CHARACTERS**

- You need to create characters for your story. One central character is fine. You may already have character profiles ready-to-go from school. Only use these if they are suitable. The best advice is to be flexible and any characters you have prepared before the exam may have to be 'tweaked' or changed a little to make them relevant and appropriate to your story. A reader wants to know what your characters look like (a few lines will do), but it is even more important to reveal their personalities. Tell the reader a little about their thoughts, feelings, disappointments, ambitions and so on. Let the characters reveal their own personality through realistic dialogue. Remember to punctuate your dialogue correctly.

- Eventually, with practice at school, you can **show the reader a character's personality traits through the character's behaviour and relationships** with others; in short, by how they act and react in different situations. This requires great skill as a writer, so do not be downhearted if you find this quite difficult at the beginning. Read as many short stories as you can and practise writing in school. Your teacher may be able to offer some good advice to help you to improve your writing skills in this area.

> Your main character should be changed by his/her experience in the story.

## THEME

- OK, so you have an idea for the setting and one or two, maybe three characters sketched out. Next, it is time to think about a theme. Ideally, your short story should explore in some way a theme: what is the key message of the story? Is it about love or friendship or poverty or betrayal and so on? In trying to decide on a theme, read the title of your short story very carefully. What comes into your head? Can you picture someone poor, someone in love, someone in trouble, someone lost, someone successful? Just write down one line about your theme – 'My story is going to be about poverty' – as this will help you to decide on a plot. Sometimes, the actual title itself will state a broad theme. At other times, it might be completely up to you!

## PLOT

- The plot is simply what happens in your short story and the order in which it happens. The examiner will expect a sense of a beginning, middle and end. In the beginning of your story, grab your reader's attention with a dramatic opening or one that hooks the reader's curiosity. Alternatively, you could open with dialogue. Land the reader in the middle of a situation. Do not write half a page of a long-winded introduction. Get straight into the action.

- In the opening section, it is also good advice to give a little background information on the setting and the main character in the story. This helps the reader to get a sense of what the story might be about and where it is occurring.

- Around the middle of your story, introduce some obstacle for your main character. Build tension by using short sentences. Once the obstacle has emerged, conflict may soon follow. The conflict may be between two people, or between a person and an organisation, or even conflict *within* the main character.

- In the climax of the story, the conflict ends. This is probably the most important paragraph in your story. It should be its key moment where conflict is resolved. It is a turning point for the main character who has learned something new about herself/himself, or about others.

## NARRATOR

- Most students decide to write their story in the third person ('he/she/they'). This is the way most stories are written and it is a good way to show what is happening in your story. Also, try a first-person narrator and see how you find it. A first-person narrator is where the story is told from the point of view of an 'I' voice.

## Other Dos and Don'ts . . .

- Do **write as many short stories in school as you can**. Feedback from your teacher and from your class can be very helpful.

- Do **plan your short story carefully**, you may have ideas and characters prepared going in, but make sure anything you write down is relevant to the title.

- Brainstorm the title.

- Do **look over the text linked with the title**, or if you have time, over all three texts; you might get ideas for a plot, or for characters or for a setting from these sources.

- Do **try to give your story its own unique title**. You can do this after planning your story, or write one down when you have completed your story.

- If you are still stuck, **write down six questions about the title** in your answer booklet. Where is the story happening? Who is involved? When did the action occur? What exactly happened? Why did it happen? How did it happen? Quickly brainstorming answers to these simple six questions might help you to get your creativity going.

- **Do not rewrite a 'ready-to-go story'** from school to fit the title if it is not directly relevant to the title. The examiner expects to see evidence of creativity and originality on the day.

- In terms of length, **three to four pages is acceptable**. One-and-a-half pages is just too short, no matter how well it is written. Obviously, you must plan your short story if you are going to be able to write up to four A4 pages on the title in just over an hour. Don't write more than 1,000 words.

## From the Exam Papers

Read the composing title below from the 2008 paper. Underline or highlight the key terms of the title. Work out *what* you have to write, *who* you are writing for, and *why* you are writing. These three factors will help you to decide *how* to write your short story.

Make a plan and then write your short story. Compare your answer with the sample short story on page 150.

---

**SECTION II**
**COMPOSING (100 marks)**

Write a composition on **any one** of the following.

Each composition carries 100 marks.

The composition assignments below are intended to reflect language study in the areas of information, argument, persuasion, narration, and the aesthetic use of language.

1. '…he had no choice…' (TEXT 1)

   **Write a short story which contains the above phrase.**

2. 'It's called Paradise...' (TEXT 1)

   **Write a personal account of your idea of paradise.**

3. '…breaking down barriers…' (TEXT 2)

   **Write an article for a school magazine in which you make suggestions to students on how to welcome newcomers into the school community.**

4. '…robot servants or 'house-bots' in our homes…' (TEXT 2)

   **Write a short story based on this idea.**

5. 'A special friend…' (TEXT 3)

   **Write a personal account of what friendship means to you.**

6. 'Grab life with both hands.' (TEXT 3)

   **Write the speech you would give to a group of young people on the importance of having a positive attitude towards life.**

7. **Write a narrative or short story based on one of the images in TEXT 3.**

Page 8 of 8

---

*What?* You are writing a short story. Remember, a short story is not a personal account.

*Who*? No specific target audience/readership is identified. So, your story is for an imagined audience. It could be written to appeal to any age group or interest group, it is up to you. But do keep your examiner in mind too! You want to impress him/her.

*Why?* You are writing a short story based on one image in Text 3, which should entertain the reader. Choose your image wisely. It must be one that sparks ideas in your mind, something you can be creative with; something that inspires you with an original idea. If the image does not excite you with possibilities, do not use it.

## ◎ Pictures of Irish Lifestyle

**The Spire,
O'Connell St., Dublin**
A wonderful new take on a
well-known landmark.

**A special friend from
a different world**
Shot on the west coast of Ireland, as a dolphin takes more
interest in the swimmer rather
than the other way round.

**A well-earned break**
A young girl takes a well-
earned break while clearing
up leaves.

**Grab life with both hands**
A relationship between man
and boy on Ireland's south
east coast, as they race to
avoid the incoming tide.

**Model goalie gives it extra**
The solitude and
determination of a camogie
player as she strikes the
ball with what seems like
a perfect swing.

**It's in the net**
Rock pools are still a source of
fascination to children.

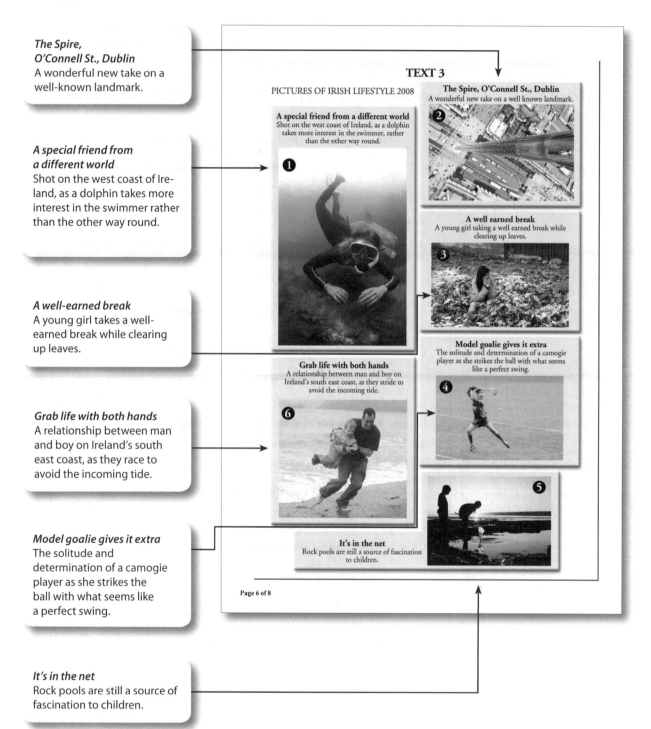

TEXT 3

PICTURES OF IRISH LIFESTYLE 2008

**The Spire, O'Connell St., Dublin**
A wonderful new take on a well known landmark.

**A special friend from a different world**
Shot on the west coast of Ireland, as a dolphin
takes more interest in the swimmer, rather
than the other way round.

**A well earned break**
A young girl taking a well earned break while
clearing up leaves.

**Model goalie gives it extra**
The solitude and determination of a camogie
player as she strikes the ball with what seems
like a perfect swing.

**Grab life with both hands**
A relationship between man and boy on
Ireland's south east coast, as they stride to
avoid the incoming tide.

**It's in the net**
Rock pools are still a source of fascination
to children.

Page 6 of 8

## ◉ Student's Answer Plan

**Introduction**

- Main character ready to dive.

- Bronwyn Evans – main character – background info – link with Titanic.

- Describe setting: Titanic caught on camera by submersible.

- Bronwyn dives and recalls her conflict with her father over college.

- Huge preparation and sacrifices she made getting ready for this day.

- Background info on Michael Evans: third class passenger, married, one child.

- Bronwyn inside the submersible; first glimpse of the wreck.

**Conclusion**

- Bronwyn's final reflections and 'discovery'.

**Note on language:** Strike up a chatty, familiar tone; try to create the effect of a one-to-one conversation with the reader. Information, description and narration are important. Also, use discursive/persuasive language. Use occasional simile/metaphor (aesthetic language).

## ◉ Sample Short Story: Image 1

### Discovery

Twenty seconds, pause for breath. Last check of equipment. Thumbs up from her dad. Then 10, 9, 8, 7 she took a deep breath then pulled her oxygen mask over her head. . . 6, 5, 4 . . . she gave a big thumbs up to her dad Gerard at the wheel . . . 3, 2, 1. She eased herself into the eerie, grey waters of the Atlantic and disappeared as gracefully as a seal. She was gone.

At 18, Bronwyn Evans vowed to her father and to herself that she would one day return to the site of her great grandfather's death. She had gathered more and more information since she was first told of the tragic loss on her father's side. Now, 10 years later, after much fundraising and several agonising delays, she was about to come face to face with the gravesite of her long lost relative; the grave of the *Titanic* in the icy waters of the north Atlantic, the grave of Michael Evans on 15 April 1912.

Most of the diving team had already seen the wreck at the bottom, 4,000 metres below the surface of the ocean. Earlier that morning, they emerged from *Stingray*, their tiny yellow submersible, filled with excitement and extraordinary video footage of what was once the greatest ship on earth. Her steel frame looked like the decaying ribs of a great mammoth while her huge propellers lay motionless, like a discarded child's toy. An uneasy current drifted past with seaweed, tangling with strands of bubbles that blew from *Stingray*. The footage was truly remarkable.

Staring at the monitor, Bronwyn could sense that the great ship still clung to her dignity, despite the severe winter storms that endlessly blew in from the Arctic and Newfoundland for almost 100 years.

But Bronwyn just had to see the ship for herself. Her father urged her to take the submersible straight away.
'No, Dad. I need to dive first, I need to feel those waters around me. Then I'll make for Stingray.' Her father understood. For many years now he noted his daughter's continuing fascination with the sinking of the Titanic. He saw it become an obsession. After school, Bronwyn dropped out of first year in college, unable to concentrate on her studies. Instead of reading her psychology books, she was in the library, researching the Titanic on the internet.
'I don't like college anyway, Dad, it bores me.' She had had a huge argument with her father when she arrived home from college for the last time.
'And what are you going to do with your life? Bum around here all year. Bronwyn, you can't waste your life doing nothing, living off social welfare, living off me.'
'Don't worry Dad, I won't live off you, you're only the humble soundman for a morning radio show, not the actual presenter.'

That hurt, and it was meant to.

But that was all forgotten now, buried in the past. Brownyn tried her best to support herself and took a variety of jobs: waitressing, childminding, painting even, anything to earn some money. Unlike other young adults, she rarely night-clubbed, didn't extend her small circle of friends, but saved as much money as she could. Her only passion was diving and every weekend she attended a diving school off the coast of Co. Mayo. Of course, there were days, weeks even, when she wondered was she mad, and she doubted what she was doing with her life. Nonetheless, after almost ten years of odd-jobs and the occasional hand-out from her dad, she finally raised the €20,000 needed to hire Stingray and her crew for three days.

Now, as she slipped easily through the shoals of fish near the surface, she knew it had all been worth it. She knew this was her chance to make that connection with her great-grandfather Michael Evans. Michael was only a young man of 22 when he boarded the Titanic in Cobh, a humble carpenter, bound for America and a new life. From what Bronwyn could gather, he was leaving behind a young wife, aged 19, and one baby boy, her grandfather. A third-class passenger, he didn't stand a chance of surviving the tragedy but perished in the dark cold waters with hundreds of others.

After 10 minutes of a dive, *Stingray* moved into position. Bronwyn climbed into the tiny capsule for the final descent to the wreck. Her heart throbbed inside her wetsuit. She gasped as she removed her oxygen mask. She peered into the darkening waters through the small viewing panel on *Stingray*. The automated cameras followed the beam projected from the submersible's powerful lights. But Bronwyn didn't look at the television monitors. Somehow, the pictures did not seem real on the monitor. Instead, she stared anxiously through the glass panel of *Stingray*, her mind bubbling with excitement inside.

Finally, she saw it. It was an overwhelming emotion. All she could do was cry, like she had never cried before. Years of hard work, of sacrifice, years of bickering with her dad over her directionless life, were now behind her. This was where her great-grandfather Michael Evans breathed his last. This was the place of his last cry, his last touch of another desperate hand, his last thought of his young wife and their beautiful baby boy. Last and then lost. Until now. Suddenly, every doubt, every moment of self-questioning that Bronwyn ever had was silenced. From the bottom of the Atlantic, the bottom of her heart, Bronwyn Evans had finally discovered what she had always been searching for: herself.

## Answering Techniques

- Begin the story in the 'middle' of the action. **No long introductions.** Grab the reader's interest and curiosity with a 'hook'.

- Give some background information.

- **Use vivid descriptive writing.** Occasionally try to include imagery (note the similes in paragraph 3).

- The third-person narrator knows what is going through Bronwyn's mind and shares this with the reader.

- **Dialogue brings the characters to life**, but do not overdo it. Note the correct way to punctuate dialogue. Also, each time you introduce a different speaker, you must go onto a new line.

- Conflict between Bronwyn and her father is recalled from the past.

- More information about Bronwyn's character tells us that she is a determined person; in the story, her actions show us that she is.

- Tension builds as Bronwyn is about to reach her goal. Note the use of shorter sentences.

- The conclusion should be **believable and convincing**.

# Key Exam Tips

## Key Exam Tips and Techniques for Composing

- You only answer one of the composition titles.

- Do not rush into this decision. Take your time. Brainstorm two titles if you are unsure of which one to do.

- On your exam paper, write down your time allowance for this question, beside the actual question.

- Read the title, at least twice. After your first reading, underline the key words in the title.

- Then work out exactly what you have to write (e.g. narrative, personal account, short story) who you are writing for (audience, if specified) and why you are writing (purpose: to entertain, to inform and so on).

- This will help you to understand how you should write your answer, what kind of language and vocabulary to use and what tone to create (register).

- Once you understand clearly the question's instructions, you must plan your answer. Spend at least five minutes at planning, 10 if needed. It is time very well spent.

- In preparing a plan, you may use ideas from one or all of the comprehending texts.

- Look at your plan. Make sure it deals with each part of the question. Start to write your full answer only after completing your plan.

- In writing your answer, remain focused on following the instructions. Do not drift off the point.

- If useful ideas come into your head while in the middle of an answer, you may be able to include these – your plan, after all, should be flexible.

- Try to give your writing an appropriate shape or structure. For example, if writing a newspaper or magazine article, use a headline and by-line. Sub-headings may also be used. At the very least, use paragraphs! If writing a short story, remember to give a sense of a beginning, middle and end. Use dialogue and punctuate it properly.

- Write at least three A4 pages. There is no need to write five or six pages. Around four pages should be a 'maximum' length.

- Remember the key point about PCLM: *what* you write is important, but *how* you write will also earn you marks. Write clearly and legibly, and pay attention to accurate spelling and grammar. And – it is worth mentioning yet again – use paragraphs!

## ◉ Record of What I Have Learned Revising for Paper 1, Section 2, Composing

**Main tips to remember when writing:**

● **A talk or more formal speech**

  ▪ _____

  ▪ _____

  ▪ _____

  ▪ _____

● **A personal narrative**

  ▪ _____

  ▪ _____

  ▪ _____

  ▪ _____

● **A personal account**

  ▪ _____

  ▪ _____

  ▪ _____

  ▪ _____

● **A short story**

  ▪ _____

  ▪ _____

  ▪ _____

  ▪ _____

Tips to help me decide which title to write on include:

- _____

- _____

- _____

- _____

Main things I must remember while answering the composing question:

● **Before writing my answer**

- _____

- _____

- _____

- _____

● **While writing my answer**

- _____

- _____

- _____

- _____

● **After writing my answer**

- _____

- _____

- _____

- _____

Well done on completing this section and completing your revision for Paper 1! In our next chapter, we move on to Paper 2, Section I, the Single Text.

**Date completed:** _____

# Your Last Minute Revision!

## Around 10 Minutes Revision for Each Study Card

● Revise your Study Cards. You will find these on the following pages:

## Around 20 Minutes Revision
(for each worked exam paper)

It would be a good idea to study again the four key steps to take in improving your composing skills.

- **Step 1**
  Reread the way questions were broken down, underlined/highlighted in this section. Make sure you know what you have to write, who you are writing for, and why you are writing. This will help you to work out how to use language in your answer – what type of vocabulary to use, and what type of tone to create. If no audience is specified, you can write for any audience of your choosing. But keep your examiner in mind too!

- **Step 2**
  Reread the sample answer plans in this section. Decide whether your plan in the exam will be a linear plan or a spider diagram.

- **Step 3**
  Reread the sample answers in this section.

- **Step 4**
  Reread the answering techniques after each sample answer.

## Check your Time Management

● Suggested timing for this section:

- Paper 1, Section II, Composing (100 marks) overall time allowance = at least 75 minutes (includes reading time and planning time).

# Paper 2

- Paper 2, Section I – The Single Text

- Paper 2, Section II – The Comparative Study

- Paper 2, Section III – Poetry

# Chapter 5

## Paper 2, Sec. I – The Single Text

This chapter contains the following sections. You should tick the boxes as you complete each section.

- Introduction ☐
- RPTA: Key Tips to Maximise Your Marks ☐
- Revision 1: The Storyline ☐
- Single Text: Revision Sheet 1 ☐
- Revision 2: Characters and Relationships ☐
- Single Text: Revision Sheet 2 ☐
- Revision 3: Personal Response ☐
- Single Text: Revision Sheet 3 ☐
- Sample Answers to 10-mark Question ☐
- Sample Answers to 30-mark Question ☐
- Key Exam Tips ☐
- Your Last Minute Revision! ☐

# Introduction

The Single Text answer must be detailed. A vague recollection of the story or the characters or a theme or two is just not good enough. There is no substitute for reading your text closely and rereading particular scenes or chapters that are most significant and revealing.

The Exam Trends in this chapter are a good place to start. They show the types of questions that have been asked on the Single Text for the past ten years or more.

Study the trends. They will give a firm direction and focus to your revision. There are also suggested revision tasks in this chapter that would be very useful to follow.

The sample answers illustrate how to plan, structure and address the Single Text question, a question that often has two, three, even four aspects to it. Each aspect of the question must be attempted in order to gain high marks.

## Overview of Paper 2

Total Marks:      200
Time Allowed:   3 hours 20 minutes

### How Many Marks, How Much Time?

Allow 10 minutes to read the paper and familiarise yourself with the options.
- Section I, the Single Text, 60 Marks (55 Minutes)
- Section II, the Comparative Study, 70 Marks (60 Minutes)
- Section III, Poetry, 70 Marks (65 Minutes)

Allow 10 minutes at the end to recheck your work.

## At a Glance

### What Must I Answer in Section I – The Single Text?

- You must answer the questions on **one** of the Single Texts on the exam paper.
- There is an index of each Single Text on the front cover of your question paper. Find the page number for the text you have studied in school and turn directly to that page.
- Answer all of the questions on that text. Expect three short questions, each worth 10 marks.
- The final question is a longer question worth 30 marks. You will be given a choice of three longer questions and you answer one of them.
- Do not waste time reading the questions on the other Single Texts.
- And do not decide on the day to 'try' the questions on a different Single Text that you might have read in Second or Third Year, or even in Transition Year.
- Stick with the Single Text you have studied and prepared for in Fifth and Sixth Years.

### General Advice

- **Avoid writing a long summary** of your chosen text. Focus on the detail required by the question instead. Many of the 10-mark questions involve information recall. To answer these, focus on providing the facts that are required.
- Where your opinion or evaluation is required, refer closely to the text in support of your points.
- The longer question (30 marks) may ask you to engage in an imaginative way with your Single Text. Be prepared for this.
- Make sure you can write out the correct title (and spelling) of your chosen text and the author's name.
- Some of the Single Texts are novels; others are plays. Make sure you refer to your Single Text correctly as either a novel or play.

# RPTA

## Key Tips to Maximise your Marks

RPTA:
Read
Plan
Time
Answer

###  Key Tip 1: READ the Question Correctly

● By now, you should be very aware that time spent reading and rereading the question is time well spent. This is extremely important in the longer 30-mark question. However, it is equally important in each of the shorter 10-mark questions. You cannot afford to lose marks because you misread the question.

> If your answer is irrelevant, you will lose marks!
> Therefore, read each question at least three times, then underline or highlight the key terms in that question.

### Key Tip 2: PLAN Your Answer

● Making a plan is a sensible thing to do. This is very important for a 30-mark question, where you have to write around one A4 page of an answer. Even with the shorter 10-mark questions, where you write approximately 10–15 lines, jot down three or four key points that you want to make in your answer and focus on these while you write.

> Do not go off the point! Use a simple plan as a guide to keep you focused.
> You must plan for a long question such as the 30-mark question – here you will write about one A4 page, perhaps four or five paragraphs.
> Plan your key point for each paragraph.

### Key Tip 3: TIME Your Answer

Time Allowed (Paper 1):
3 Hours 20 Minutes

● The suggested time for the Single Text question is 55 minutes.
This includes reading time and planning time.

## Key Tip 4: ANSWER the Question Asked

● Just before you begin to write your full answer, look once again at the question, then at your plan. Double check that the points in your plan will answer the key instructions in the question. Tweak your plan a little if you need to. This might only take a minute or less. Note again your time allowance for the question, then begin.

# Revision 1

## The Storyline

You need a good understanding of the storyline or plot. Know the order of important events in the novel or play. Reread key scenes in your novel or play as often as possible.

**Suggested revision tasks:**

● In about 200 words, outline the plot of the text.

● Describe the text's setting (time and place).

● Describe two significant events from the opening, two from the middle and two from the closing chapters, scenes or sections of the text. (See the revision sheets in this chapter.)

● Reread any chapter or scenes where significant conflict occurred. Know what happened, why it happened, who was involved and how it was resolved.

---

**HINT**

For 10-mark questions, write about 150 words – around half a page.
Jot down three or four key points that you want to make before you begin writing an answer.
Use paragraphs.

---

## Questions Asking You to Describe or Analyse a Significant Moment or Event in Your Single Text

**Novel Questions (10 marks)**

● What circumstances caused Eve Malone to go to live in the convent with Mother Francis? (*Circle of Friends*)

● Describe what happens when Nick Carraway first visits Tom and Daisy Buchanan at their home. (*The Great Gatsby*)

● Describe Jim's life in Shanghai before the war. (*Empire of the Sun*)

● Describe the occasion when Jack and his parents take a trip around Dublin Bay on the Royal Iris. (*Home Before Night*)

● Why does Charlotte Lucas agree to marry Mr Collins? (*Pride and Prejudice*)

- Describe one horrible experience that Alec endures in the war-zone. (*How Many Miles to Babylon?*)

- Describe what happens when Mr Earnshaw brings Heathcliff home to Wuthering Heights. (*Wuthering Heights*)

- Give a brief account of one issue raised by Br Benedict during his meeting with Br Sebastian at the beginning of the novel. (*Lamb*)

- Describe the reactions of Michael and Moira when the IRA men enter their home. (*Lies of Silence*)

- Describe the occasion when Tom Joad, on his way home from McAlester Prison, meets Preacher Casey. (*The Grapes of Wrath*)

- Briefly describe the party in Helen's house at the beginning of the novel. (*The Blackwater Lightship*)

- Describe the scene early in the novel when Christopher is arrested and brought to the police station. (*The Curious Incident of the Dog in the Night-time*)

- Describe what happened on the last evening/night before Alec and Jerry joined the army. (*How Many Miles to Babylon?*)

**Drama Questions (10 marks)**

- Describe the occasion, as told by the guard, when Antigone buries the body of her brother, Polynices. (*Antigone*)

- What are Jerry Devine and Mary arguing about in Act I? *(Juno and the Paycock)*

- 'Yet she must die, else she'll betray more men.' Describe the murder of Desdemona by Othello in Act 5, scene 2. *(Othello)*

- Describe how the matchmaker convinces Mena that Sive should marry Sean Dota. *(Sive)*

- Describe what happens in Act 1 when Nora and Jack are alone after Peter and the Covey have gone out for the evening. (*The Plough and the Stars*)

- From your reading of the play, why do you think Fr Jack was sent home from Africa? (*Dancing at Lughnasa*)

- Describe how Mena plans to arrange a match for Sive. (*Sive*)

- How does Cordelia upset her father at the beginning of the play? *(King Lear)*

- Describe what happened during the visit of the Americans (Aunt Lizzy, Uncle Con and Ben Burton) to the O'Donnell household. (*Philadelphia, Here I Come!*)

- Why is Reverend Parris so upset and angry at the beginning of the play? (*The Crucible*)

- Describe the actions taken by Lady Macbeth when she attempts to conceal the fact that Macbeth has murdered King Duncan. *(Macbeth)*

##  Answering Tips!

- To answer questions such as these, you need to have a good knowledge of the storyline of your Single Text. There is no substitute for reading your novel, or closely studying your play (and, if possible, viewing a performance of your play). You must be familiar with the main events in the plot. If you studied your novel or play in Fifth Year, you should reread it again in Sixth Year. Otherwise, much of the material could be very vague in your head. Obviously, you are not expected to remember everything that happens in your text, so focus on the main events and the key scenes.

- Secondly, these are 10-mark questions, so a detailed response is not expected. However, this is all the more reason to remain focused on the question – there is little room for padding or waffle in such a short answer. Everything you write down must be relevant.

- Look at the instructions in the above questions. Most ask you to describe something that happened in your text. Therefore, do not explain *why* it happened (unless asked to do so).

- Use the template on the next page to make notes on your Single Text that might help you to prepare for answering a question on a particular moment or event in your novel or play.

# Single Text Revision Sheet 1
## Notes Linked with Key Events/Scenes

Student's Name: _____ Date: _____

Novel/Play: _____ Author/Playwright: _____

Opening Section ☐            Middle Section ☐            Closing Section ☐

Describe two events, incidents, moments or scenes from the opening, middle or closing section of your Single Text that you thought were memorable, moving, frightening, dramatic, amusing or significant in any way. Write about 150 words on each event.

● 1

Page reference in text: ☐

● **Key Quotations**
- ■ _____
- ■ _____

● 2

Page reference in text: ☐

● **Key Quotations**
- ■ _____
- ■ _____

Photocopy this sheet and use it to make notes on significant events or scenes while revising the opening, middle and closing sections of your Single Text.

# Revision 2

## Characters and Relationships

Focus your revision on characters, their relationships and how they change during the novel/play.

**Suggested revision tasks:**

● Make a list of the main characters in your novel or play.

● Prepare a brief physical description of each of them.

● Prepare a paragraph on the type of person they are in the text.

● Describe the role of each character in the text. What was their main function? What did they do?

● Describe two important relationships they had in the text. Were these relationships positive or negative?

● Describe one key event in which each main character was involved.

● Outline how each character changes (if they do change) from the beginning to the ending of the novel or play.

● Describe in about 100 words, why you like or dislike each character.

  ▪ Aim to write about one A4 page of notes on each of the main characters in your Single Text. These notes will be helpful when answering a 10-mark or even a 30-mark question on a character.

  ▪ You may photocopy the Revision Sheet 2 on page 170 if it is helpful and use it to make notes on key characters. Keep the completed notes on file in a ring-binder.

> **HINT**
> For 10-mark questions, write about 150 words – around half a page. Jot down three or four key points you want to make before you begin writing an answer. Use paragraphs. More in-depth character analysis is required for a 30-mark question; see Revision 3 below.

## ◉ Questions Asking Your Opinion of the Characters, their Actions and their Relationships in a Novel or Play

### Novel Questions (10 marks)

- Do you think Eve Malone is a good friend to Benny? Give one reason for your answer. (*Circle of Friends*)

- Do you think that the relationship between Alec and his mother was good or bad? Give one reason for your answer. (*How Many Miles to Babylon?*)

- Alec admits that he lacked 'team spirit'. Do you think that he would have been a more successful person if he had been sent to school? Explain your answer. (*How Many Miles to Babylon?*)

- Explain what you find most interesting about Basie, the American man Jim meets several times during the course of the novel. (*Empire of the Sun*)

- In your opinion, why is Benny's first dress dance so important for her? Support your answer with reference to the novel. (*Circle of Friends*)

- In your opinion, do Tom and Daisy Buchanan have a happy marriage? Support your answer with reference to the novel. (*The Great Gatsby*)

- What is your opinion of Jack's adoptive mother, Margaret? Support your answer with reference to the text. (*Home Before Night*)

- Why do you think Major Glendinning dislikes Alec? Support your answer with reference to the novel. (*How Many Miles to Babylon?*)

- From your reading of the novel, do you think that Charlotte is happy in her marriage to Mr Collins? Explain your answer. (*Pride and Prejudice*)

### Drama Questions (10 marks)

- What is your opinion of Sean Dota? Support your answer with reference to the play. (*Sive*)

- In your opinion, is Lady Macbeth a good influence on Macbeth? Support your answer with reference to the play. (*Macbeth*)

- Do you think that Jerry Devine does the right thing in rejecting Mary when he discovers she is pregnant by Bentham? Explain your answer. (*Juno and the Paycock*)

- From your reading of the play, why do you think Desdemona falls in love with Othello? Explain your answer. (*Othello*)

- Do you think that Mike, Mena's husband, is a weak man? Explain your answer. (*Sive*)

- Do you like Sive's grandmother, Nanna Glavin? Explain your answer with reference to the text. (*Sive*)

**HINT** In answering on your play, you are free to support the points you make with references to performances of the text that you have seen.

- Do you think that King Lear was wise to banish Kent? Explain your answer. (*King Lear*)

- Do you like Edmund? Explain your answer with reference to the text. (*King Lear*)

- In your opinion, was Gar a good son to S.B. O'Donnell? Give reasons for your answer. (*Philadelphia, Here I Come!*)

- In your view, was Elizabeth Proctor a good wife to John Proctor? Explain your answer, by reference to the play. (*The Crucible*)

## ◉ Answering Tips!

- You can possibly see that these questions are quite different to the 'what happened' style of question. In answering these questions, you must **give your opinion**.

- Make sure that your opinions on characters are based on evidence in the novel or play you studied. Whether you think a character is evil-minded or kind-hearted, a good father or a poor husband and so on, you must be able to go into the text and pull out evidence to support your viewpoint. A 10-mark question does not require a very detailed analysis of the character here. **Focus on the character's personality and actions.** Nonetheless, you must explain your answer with reference to the text. High marks will be awarded to answers that include valid and interesting evidence from the text to support the points made.

- Remember that information from the text used to support your **answer must be accurate** and relevant to the question.

## Single Text Revision Sheet 2
## Notes Linked with My Personal Response to Characters

Student's Name: _____ Date: _____

Novel/Play: _____ Author/Playwright: _____

Character's Name: _____

Physical description: _____

_____

● **What does he/she 'do' in the text?**

● **Outline this character's main relationships in the text.**

Relationship 1:



Relationship 2:



● **Describe one key event/scene in which this character was involved.**

● **Explain why you like or dislike this character. Refer closely to the novel or play in support of your opinions.**

Photocopy this sheet and use it to make notes on significant characters while revising the opening, middle and closing sections of your Single Text.

# Revision 3

## Personal Response (30-mark question)

Focus on your overall, personal response to the story of a novel or play, its main theme, and its main characters.

**Suggested revision tasks:**

● Study your character sketches from Revision 2.

● Prepare one A4 page on one key theme of the novel or play.

● Write one page on your overall impression of the text – why you enjoyed it, your favourite scenes and so on.

● Briefly revise the Study Cards for Paper 1, Section I, Question B on writing a **diary**, **letter**, or **talk**, and a **newspaper/magazine article**.

### Questions Asking for Your Understanding of the Text's Characters, Themes, Setting, Atmosphere

> **HINT**
> Three 30-mark questions will appear on the exam paper. You answer one of the three. More detail is expected for a 30-mark question. Write between 300 and 500 words, about one to one-and-a-half A4 pages. Plan your answer. Use paragraphs. Leave a few minutes at the end to check over your work. You can expect that one of the three questions will ask for an imaginative and creative response.

**Novel Questions**
### Character analysis (30 marks)

● 'Gatsby is a very mysterious and unusual character.' Do you agree with the above statement? Give reasons for your answer, based on your knowledge of the text. *(The Great Gatsby)*

● Write a piece about the friendship between Alec and Jerry, explaining why you think this friendship is so important in the novel. Support your answer with reference to the text. *(How Many Miles to Babylon?)*

● 'Jack's childhood and youth are mostly happy'.
Do you agree with the above statement? Give reasons for your answer, based on your knowledge of the text. *(Home Before Night)*

● A student said: 'Mr Darcy is a far more interesting man than Mr Bingley.' If you were to choose one of these men as your friend, which one would it be? Explain your answer with reference to the novel. *(Pride and Prejudice)*

- 'Benny is a very sensible girl.'
  Write a piece, based on this statement. You might refer to her decisions, her actions and her relationships with others, etc. in the course of the novel. (*Circle of Friends*)

- Write a piece beginning with one of the following statements:

  - I feel sorry for Heathcliff because . . .

  - I never really liked Heathcliff because . . .

- Your response should be based on your understanding of the novel. (*Wuthering Heights*)

- 'Cordelia is a fascinating character.' Do you agree with this view of her? Support your answer by reference to the novel. (*Cat's Eye*)

- Do you agree that Helen O'Doherty is an unhappy character in this novel? Give reasons for your answer. (*The Blackwater Lightship*)

## Overall response to the novel (30 marks)

- Write a piece, beginning with one of the following statements:

  - I think the world of this novel is glamorous and exciting.

  - I think the world of this novel is dangerous and unpleasant.

  Support your answer with reference to the text. (*The Great Gatsby*)

- Some readers find Maeve Binchy's novel, *Circle of Friends*, more interesting because it is set in two very different places, Knockglen and Dublin. Would you agree? Support your answer with reference to the text. (*Circle of Friends*)

- Write a piece, beginning with one of the following statements:

  - I think Ireland today is very different from the Ireland of Jack's youth.

  - I think Ireland today is very similar to the Ireland of Jack's youth.

  Support your answer with reference to the text. (*Home Before Night*)

- Write an article about Emily Bronte's *Wuthering Heights* for your school magazine in which you consider whether the novel is relevant to young people today. (*Wuthering Heights*)

## Imaginative response (30 marks)

**N.B. Your answer must be based on characters, events and situations that occur in the novel.**

- If you could become one of the characters in the novel *Circle of Friends*, which character would you choose to be? Explain your answer with reference to the novel. (*Circle of Friends*)

- Imagine you are Jack, now an old man. Write a letter to one of your childhood friends in which you comment on some of the important events of your youth. Your response should be based on your knowledge of the novel. (*Home Before Night*)

● Imagine you are Nick Carraway. Write two diary entries: one after you meet Gatsby for the first time and another after his funeral, in which you reflect on his life. You should base your response on your knowledge of the novel. *(The Great Gatsby)*

● Imagine you are a soldier in Alec and Jerry's regiment. Write a letter home in which you give a brief account of what happened to both Alec and Jerry at the end of the story. Your letter should include your views on what happened to each character. Your response should be based on your knowledge of the novel. *(How Many Miles to Babylon?)*

● Letters are an important source of information in *Pride and Prejudice*. Imagine you are a guest of Lady Catherine de Bourgh. Write a letter to a friend, describing the time you spent there and the people you met. *(Pride and Prejudice)*

> **HINT**
>
> Note that the questions inviting a more imaginative and creative answer often ask you to perform a functional writing task, e.g. write a newspaper or magazine article, a letter, a diary, or a short talk. Use the skills you have developed from revising Paper 1 while answering.

## Drama Questions
### Character analysis (30 marks)

● 'In the play *Juno and the Paycock*, the women are the ones who offer us most hope for the future.' Discuss this view in the light of your knowledge of the play. *(Juno and the Paycock)*

● 'Sive's life is tragic.'
Do you agree with the above statement? Give reasons for your answer, based on your knowledge of the text. *(Sive)*

● 'Lady Macbeth is the real villain of the play.'
Do you agree with the above statement? Give reasons for your answer, based on your knowledge of the text. *(Macbeth)*

● At the very end of the play, Lodovico describes Iago as a hellish villain. Do you think this is a fair description of Iago? Support your answer with reference to the play. *(Othello)*

### Overall response to the play: theme, setting, etc. (30 marks)

● Write a review of *Juno and the Paycock* in which you advise your readers to attend or not to attend a performance of the play. *(Juno and the Paycock)*

● Write a report putting forward the view that Othello is, or is not, a suitable text for Leaving Certificate candidates. *(Othello)*

● Write a piece, beginning with the following phrase:
'I find the world of this play hopeless and depressing because. . .'
Support your answer with reference to the text. *(Sive)*

● Shakespeare's use of horror and the supernatural added to my enjoyment of the play, Macbeth. Support your answer with reference to the play. *(Macbeth)*

- Write a piece about the play, *Dancing at Lughnasa*, beginning with one of the following statements:

  - I enjoyed this play because . . .

  - I did not enjoy this play because . . . (*Dancing at Lughnasa*)

- Based on your reading of the play, write a piece beginning with one of the following statements:

  - This is a story about foolishness.

  - This is a story about love. (*King Lear*)

- 'Lack of communication is the main problem for the characters in *Philadelphia, Here I Come!*' Do you agree? In your answer, you should refer to one or more of the characters in the play. (*Philadelphia, Here I Come!*)

> Do not write a summary of the whole novel or play in answering a 30-mark question. Long, extensive, unfocused summaries are not awarded high marks. Focus instead on characters, scenes, events, or moments in the text that illustrate your key points most effectively.

- 'Arthur Miller's play, *The Crucible*, is so cruel that it is unsuitable for study by Leaving Certificate students.' Discuss this view, referring to events from the play in your answer. (*The Crucible*)

- This play is set in Salem in 1692. Would you like to have lived there at that time? Support the points you make by reference to the play. (*The Crucible*)

## Imaginative response (30 marks)

**N.B. Your answer must be based on characters, events and situations that occur in the play.**

- Imagine that you are Mary at the end of the play. Write two diary entries revealing your attitude to Charles Bentham. (*Juno and the Paycock*)

- You have been invited to play the part of a character in a production of the play *Othello*. Describe the qualities of your chosen character which you would wish to make clear to your audience. Support your answer with reference to the text. (*Othello*)

- Imagine you are Sive. Write two diary entries: one, after you learn that you must marry Sean Dota, and a second when you believe Liam Scuab has abandoned you. You should base your response on your knowledge of the play. (*Sive*)

- Imagine you are a Scottish noble. Write a letter to a friend who lives abroad. In your letter, outline what life is like now that Macbeth is King and express your hopes for Scotland's future. You should base your letter on your knowledge of the play. (*Macbeth*)

- Imagine you are a newspaper reporter. Write a piece in which you describe the shooting and looting taking place in Dublin during the Easter rising. Your response should be based on information drawn from the play. (*The Plough and the Stars*)

● Write the letter Chris Mundy might have written to Gerry Evans, beginning with the following statement:
'Dear Gerry,
I'm writing to you to explain why I won't marry you.'
*(Dancing at Lughnasa)*

● Imagine you are Madge, the housekeeper in the O'Donnell home. Write the letter you would send to Gar a week after he left for Philadelphia. You should refer to characters and/or events from the play in your letter. (*Philadelphia, Here I Come!*)

## Answering Tips!

● **A 30-mark question on a character requires a more detailed response than a 10-mark question.** If you are writing about your overall impression of a character in a novel or play, you need to consider the text as a whole before answering. Then you must focus on key scenes in the text that provide evidence to support your points.

● There are various types of evidence that you can use:

  ▪ You could refer to the way the character speaks to others in the text.

  ▪ You could refer to the character's **role** in the text, the things that they do, the way that they act and behave.

  ▪ You could examine the character's **attitude** towards life in general. Is the character optimistic or pessimistic about life? Does this attitude appeal to you, or even inspire you?

  ▪ Looking at a character's **background** is also interesting. The setting in which the character lives might have helped or hindered that character in the novel or play. Some characters are to be admired for overcoming obstacles and difficulties in the text's setting.

  ▪ You could look at the way the writer, narrator or playwright describes the character. Do you get the impression that the writer likes or dislikes the character, approves or disapproves of the character's **behaviour**?

> Remember! For a 30-mark question, you must support your points by accurate reference to and/or quotation from your Single Text. General, vague answers will never achieve more than a Grade D. The strength of your answer will depend on the evidence that you give.

  ▪ You could refer to the character's **relationships**, whether they are positive or negative. Try to identify where a relationship changes or develops in your Single Text. And even better, if you can understand *why* a relationship changes, you will earn high marks. How the character reacts to and interacts with other characters always reveals a good deal about the type of person he or she is.

  ▪ You could refer to the way a character copes in certain situations. Explore how the character responds to pressure, in times of conflict or crisis, or deals with moments of conflict or crisis.

## Theme

- For a question on a novel's or a play's main theme, or the issues raised in the text, you must **identify key moments or key scenes** where that theme was illustrated or developed. For example, if the theme of a text is violence, you must refer to two or three occasions in the text when violence occurred or was threatened. Then, you **discuss these and explain what they show about the key theme**.

## Imaginative response

- For a question where you have to write a letter, diary, newspaper or magazine article, etc., use the writing skills that you developed while studying for Paper 1. You can also use your imagination in answering this question. However, remember that your answer must be based on the actual text; therefore, include references to events, incidents, setting and characters in the text in your answer. **Use material from the text in a creative and imaginative way.**

## The play on stage

- If you are asked to play the part of one character on stage, there are different areas that you can write about:

  - Try to remain true to the character's feelings and values in the original play. Write about the main feelings this character had in the play and why you would like to act out such feelings on stage.

  - Write about the facial expressions that you imagine this character would have to show on stage. Explain why this would be challenging or fun for you to try to dramatise on stage.

  - Write about the key relationships that this character would have. What would you find interesting about acting with other main characters in the play?

  - Write about the type of costume that you might have to wear. Explain why you would wear such a costume and how it reflects your character or role on stage.

  - Consider how you would speak on stage and where you would position yourself on stage.

- If you are asked to direct a scene from the play, consider writing about:

  - The stage set: what props would you want to see on stage? How could you ensure the props are appropriate to the original play's setting (time and place)? What scenery would you want behind the actors? Describe and explain why you would choose such scenery.

  - What type of actors would you choose to play the main parts? Would they be timid, forceful, confident, aggressive, villainous and so on? Explain why you would select such actors.

  - Think about the lighting that you might use. Describe and explain the use of floodlights or spotlights, or any special lighting effects that you might use in the scene.

  - What about using music or sound effects in the scene? Describe what you would use and explain why you would use these sound effects. What would they add to the scene? Would they help to create an appropriate atmosphere, or create an emotive effect on the audience?

# Single Text Revision Sheet 3
## Notes on the Text's Main Theme and My Overall Response

Student's Name: _____ Date: _____

Novel/Play: _____ Author/Playwright: _____

- **In one line, write down one main theme of the novel/play.**

- **Briefly, write down what the text has to 'say' about this theme.**

- **Describe any three scenes in the text, where this theme was explored or developed.**

Scene 1:

Scene 2:

Scene 3:

- **Describe your overall response to the text. Say why you liked/disliked it. Refer to the text in support of your points.**

Photocopy this sheet and use it to make notes on your overall response while revising the opening, middle and closing sections of your Single Text.

# Sample Answers to 10-mark Questions

On the following pages, you will see a selection of sample answers to 10-mark questions from past exam papers.

> Remember RPTA that you used for Paper 1.
> Read the question carefully. Plan your answer.
> Know your Time allowance. Double check that you are about
> to Answer the question that is asked.

Read these sample answers to get an idea about how to structure your response to a 10-mark question.

- For your Single Text, aim to write about 150 words (half an A4 page) when answering a 10-mark question.

- Use two or three paragraphs.

- Don't write more than one A4 page.

## 2009: Paper 2, Section I, The Single Text

*The Curious Incident of the Dog in the Night-time* – Mark Haddon
Do you like or dislike Christopher's mother, Judy Boone? Explain your answer. (10 marks)

### Judy Boone

I do not really like Judy Boone very much. I think Judy loved Christopher, but she was unable to cope with his behavioural problems. For example, Christopher tells us that sometimes when he clashed with his mother, she would shout at him, threatening him: 'Jesus, Christopher, I am seriously considering putting you in a home.' I think this is a very hurtful thing to say, no matter what kind of pressure Christopher put her under. She is, after all, his mother.

Furthermore, Christopher remarks that his father rarely grabbed his arm tightly, whereas his mother had struck him several times. He describes her as a 'very hot-tempered person' who 'had hit me sometimes'. I do not approve of her use of physical violence against Christopher. I think she was selfish and lashed out at Christopher when the pressure got to her.

However, from one of her 43 letters to Christopher, we see her apologise to him and she claims, 'I still love you'. She also says that she thinks about Christopher 'all the time'. This does not change my opinion of her. I agree with Judy Boone herself when she writes 'I'm not a very good mother'. Her claim that things might have been different is not very gracious: 'maybe if things had been different, maybe if you'd been different'. I do not like the way she again, selfishly shifts the blame onto Christopher. I think she should have accepted Christopher for who he was, and not abandon him because of what he was.

## 2009: Paper 2, Section I, The Single Text

*The Curious Incident of the Dog in the Night-time* – Mark Haddon
What kind of a relationship does Christopher have with Siobhan, his teacher at school?
Refer to the novel in your answer. (10 marks)

## Christopher and Siobhan

Christopher has a very interesting and close relationship with Siobhan, his teacher at school. Siobhan is often very kind to Christopher. She gives him advice on many things, including on how he should write his book. For example, in the novel Christopher tells us that 'Siobhan said that when you are writing a book you have to include some descriptions of things'.

Christopher is obviously close to Siobhan. He trusts her. He lets her read his work, after which she would help Christopher by advising him if he 'had made mistakes with the spelling and the grammar'.

Siobhan also talks with Christopher about his life and his feelings. She asks if he was upset when he heard that his mother was having an affair with Mr Shears. She also stands up for Christopher. This is clear when Mrs Forbes tells Christopher that hating yellow and brown 'is just being silly'. Siobhan comforts Christopher by telling him 'she shouldn't say things like that and everyone has favourite colours'.

Further evidence of their close relationship can be seen when Christopher speaks with her soon after hitting his father. She showed genuine concern over what happened, and Christopher tells us, 'then she asked me if I wanted to talk about it any more'.

Christopher and Siobhan, therefore, have a very special, close relationship.

**2010: Paper 2, Section I, The Single Text**

*Dancing at Lughnasa* – Brian Friel
From your reading of the play, why do you think Fr Jack was sent home from Africa?
(10 marks)

## Father Jack

From my reading of the play, I think there may have been several reasons why Fr Jack was sent home from Africa.

He had spent 25 years working as a priest on the missions in Uganda, much of it in a hospice for lepers. At the beginning of the play, the narrator, Michael, tells us that he returned to Ireland out of bad health, and had come home 'to die'. He describes Jack as being 'shrunken and jaundiced with malaria' on his return in 1936.

Another reason why he returned to Ballybeg may be because of his involvement in pagan practices 'to please the spirits'. Such pagan practices would be severely frowned upon by his Christian superiors.

Jack also took part in ritual dances in Ryanga. Around fires, he danced and danced and drank wine and painted his face with 'ritual powders'. Kate lets Jack know that he has crossed a boundary that is unacceptable to Christian teaching and morals. While Jack talks with enthusiasm about offering an animal sacrifice to Obi, 'Our Great Goddess of the earth', Kate's attitude is very different: 'Leaping around a fire and offering a little hen to Uka or Ito or whoever, is not religion as I was taught it and indeed know it.'

I think Kate's shock at each new revelation would reflect the attitude of the Church who probably felt that Jack was no longer fulfilling his missionary duties in Africa and so they sent him home. At the end of the play the narrator, Michael, tells us that Jack recovered his health, but that he never said mass again. He is the one who was converted.

# Sample Answers to 30-mark Questions

On the following pages, you will see a selection of sample answers to 30-mark questions from past exam papers.

> Remember **RPTA** that you used for Paper 1.
> Read the question carefully. Plan your answer.
> Know your Time allowance. Double check that you are about
> to Answer the question that is asked.

Read these sample answers to get an idea about how to structure your response to a 30-mark question. For your Single Text, aim to write around 1½ A4 pages when answering a 30-mark question.

## 2008: Paper 2, Section I, The Single Text

*How Many Miles to Babylon?* – Jennifer Johnston
'*How Many Miles to Babylon?* is a great read.'
Write an article for a magazine, in which you support or oppose the above view of the novel.
(30 marks)

### Something for Everyone in 'Babylon'

Many of you who have been reading my recent articles on the best novels in our bookstores this year will know that I love a good story. Give me adventure, mystery, action, romance, whatever, but without a good story behind any of these genres, a novel will always fail to ignite me.

On leaving my local library last Saturday afternoon, my heart was almost on fire. I had just dropped into the library around 10 a.m. for a casual browse. By 10.30, I was three chapters into the novel *How Many Miles to Babylon?* and I just couldn't put the novel down. Nearly two hours later and I wish I could have shaken the hand of the author, Jennifer Johnston, for a job well done.

*How Many Miles to Babylon?* is a remarkable novel, a great read. Set in rural Ireland, it tells the story of Alexander Moore, his over-zealous mother Alicia, and his demoralised father, Frederick. Once Alec meets with the local, working class boy, Jeremiah Crowe, the story takes us on an adventure into the hearts and minds of two very different, yet very similar young men.

182

One reason I think the novel is such a great read is the variety of themes explored by Johnston. The theme of friendship, for example, runs strongly throughout the text. Alec tells the reader that 'As a child I was lone . . . I was isolated from the surrounding children of my own age by the traditional barriers of class and education.' When Alec met Jerry Crowe it was the beginning of a new, exciting experience for him. The tension that builds between Alicia, who demands an end to an 'unsuitable' friendship, and Alec who struggles to assert himself, is quite gripping. Despite Alicia's best efforts, the bond between the two young men strengthens as they march off to fight in the battlefields of Ypres during the First World War. As the story unfolds, Alec and Jerry forge an understanding and trust that is heart-warming and uplifting, to the dismay of Major Glendinning who wants to keep them apart.

Another theme explored in the plot is that of family life. Alec is controlled by his domineering mother while a boy, while his father sits back passively, smoking his pipe, enduring ridicule from his wife. Their husband and wife relationship is barely alive. They hardly ever talk and when they do it is usually about Alec, since 'their only meeting place was the child'. Ironically, they live in a beautiful home, surrounded by servants and expensive material things, yet behind it all there is emptiness, a bleakness, and a void. Sadly, this is why Alec reflects at the end of the novel that he 'loves no living person'.

There are twists and turns in the plot along the way that will keep you in suspense, but this novel is a gripping great read and one I can recommend without reservation. If you cannot find it in your local library (they have probably all been taken!), pop down to your local bookstore this weekend and treat yourself to your own copy. Happy reading!

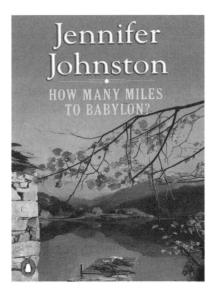

## 2009: Paper 2, Section I, The Single Text

*The Curious Incident of the Dog in the Night-time* – Mark Haddon
Imagine that Christopher's father, Ed Boone, kept a diary. Write the diary entry Ed Boone might have written after Christopher discovered the hidden letters from his mother. Support your answer with reference to the novel. (30 marks)

## Ed Boone's Diary

Diary,

What can I say? I do not know what I feel. I'm so confused after what happened today. I never thought for one moment that Christopher would discover the letters. So what now?

Looking back, I feel such a fake. From the day I pretended to Christopher that Judy had died of a heart attack – pretending to be 'so sorry' for the so-called death of his mother – I have been filling him with lies ever since. Bad days.

But there were good days too. I'll always treasure the times we went boating together on the lake and the afternoons browsing through the garden centres. Yes, there were good days.

I have to pull myself together now, I can't keep putting myself down – I need to be strong – for both of us. And I was strong for Christopher. I remember how I stood up for him at school. I complained to the school head Mrs Gascoyne, about Christopher getting a 'crap enough deal' in life. Those teachers can be so stupid sometimes. I knew that A-level maths was the one thing Christopher was really good at.

But I have done stupid things as well. It's sad that I turned Christopher against Mr Shears. I told Christopher that he was an evil man. And I shouldn't have cursed at Christopher when he was asking questions around the estate. I don't know why I called him a 'little shit'. In a way, I don't blame Christopher for hitting me when I grabbed his arm. I felt sick that night. I did apologise to him the next day, but apologies sometimes do not seem to mean much to Christopher.

Despite everything that I have messed up, I do care for my boy. I meant it when I told him in the zoo café that I loved him very much. I admitted to him that I lose my rag sometimes that I get angry and shout, but I do all this because I do not want him to get hurt.

Just after this when we both touched fingers, it was probably the closest I felt to Christopher in a long time.

I just hope that he can forgive me. I hope that one day he might understand that I hid the letters to protect him. It's funny, isn't it, that I had to tell Christopher lies to protect him from the truth; that his mother had left him and run off with Mr Shears. What else could I have done? What do I do now?

Ed.

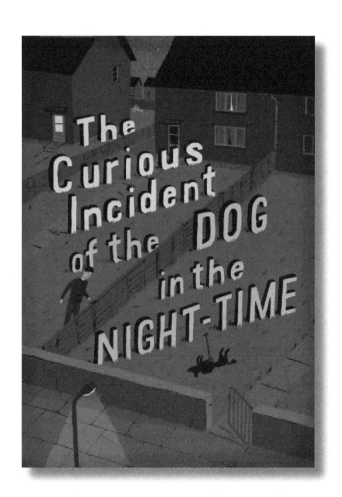

**2007: Paper 2, Section I The Single Text**

*Juno and the Paycock* – Sean O'Casey

'In the play *Juno and the Paycock*, the women are the ones who offer us most hope for the future.'

Discuss this view in light of your knowledge of the play. (30 marks)

## Hope for the Future

In the play *Juno and the Paycock*, the character of Juno is certainly the one that offers the audience most hope for the future. I find many qualities admirable in Juno throughout the play. Despite her difficult and impoverished surroundings, she is a character who is rich in her reserves of strength and determination, two qualities that are essential in the struggle to achieve a better future.

In Act 1, one of the first impressions I get of Juno is of a hardworking, practical woman. She prepares to go out to work and regrets that Mary cannot do the same. Juno is very much grounded in the real world and despite Mary's claim that 'a principle's a principle', Juno knows that principles do not pay bills: 'When I go into oul Murphy and instead of paying all, I'm going to borrow more, what'll he say when I tell him a principle's a principle?' Unlike Boyle who is a dreamer, Juno reminds the others that she is the one who has worked hard to keep the family together: 'I killing myself working and he strutting about from morning 'til night like a paycock'.

At the start of Act 2, Juno carries a gramophone onto the stage. Juno is somewhat uneasy about getting so many goods on credit. The gramophone, for example, was acquired with 'a pound down, and five to be paid at two shillings a week'. Boyle, by contrast, is happy to borrow for furniture, beer, and so on. Juno says: 'I'm afraid we're running into too much debt: first the furniture and now this.' She is cautious about the future, something perhaps many Irish people should have been during the Celtic Tiger years.

In Act 2, Juno's struggle for a better future is driven by her keen awareness of the past. She reminds Jack of the terrible consequences of violence on the tenement community around them: 'Hasn't the whole house nearly been massacred – young Dougherty's husband with his leg off; Mrs Travers' son was blown up in a mine; Mrs Mannin' lost one of her sons in an ambush; Robbie Tancred's 'body was made a colander of'.

At the beginning of Act 3, Juno shows her caring, motherly side once again. She quizzes Mary about her health and about Bentham; she is interested in her daughter's happiness, her welfare, and her future. She also advises Mary 'But you shouldn't be fretting ... When a woman loses a man, ... she never knows what she's after gaining.' Juno's spirit of never giving up, despite the chaos that surrounds her, is a beacon of hope for the future.

It is interesting that when Juno hears that the Will is 'a washout', she laments the fact that so many men are devious and untrustworthy: 'Oh, is there not even a middlin' honest man left in the world.' Juno has some very harsh words to say about men in general, and in particular about her husband, Jack Boyle. At the end of the play, she comforts Mary by saying her baby will be better off in having 'two mothers'. This shows her despair for 'fatherly' figures in the play. Similarly, she also realises that Jack will be 'hopeless till the end of his days'.

We admire Juno who, despite the hardships she has had to bear, can still pray for the help of the Sacred Heart of Jesus. Her family has worn her out, yet her final words on stage are an appeal for love. It is certainly women like Juno who offer us most hope for the future.

# Key Exam Tips!

## Key Exam Tips and Techniques for Answering on Paper 2, Section I, the Single Text

- On your exam paper, write down your time allowance for this question, beside the actual question.

- Read the question, at least twice. After your first reading, underline the key instructions.

- Once you understand clearly what the question is instructing you to do, you must plan your answer. This need only take a few minutes, but it is time very well spent.

- Write no less than half a page to answer a 10-mark question.

- Write about one to one-and-a-half pages to answer a 30-mark question.

- In writing your answer, remain focused on following the instructions. Do not drift off the point. Expect questions on the Single Text to deal with the plot, the characters, one main theme, and your overall impression of the text. Plan your answer, especially for the 30-mark question.

- Refer closely to the Single Text in support of each answer that you write.

- Include references to the text and/or use quotations from the text. Don't feel you have to quote large chunks from the text – you do not! A short phrase or line used wisely is much more effective. Two or three short quotes are fine in a 10-mark answer. In a 30-mark answer, you might be able to use five or six short quotes.

- Remember to insert quotation marks ("...") around the words/phrases that you are quoting from the novel/play.

- Don't be afraid of making a personal response, but you must refer to the text to make sure that you earn higher marks.

> **Remember!**
> You cannot use a Single Text that you have answered
> on in this section as part of your Comparative Study.

## Record of What I Have Learned Revising for Paper 2, Section I, the Single Text

**Main Tips to Remember When Writing**

- Answering the questions on the plot or storyline

  - _____
  - _____
  - _____
  - _____

- Answering the questions on the main characters

  - _____
  - _____
  - _____
  - _____

- Answering the 30-mark question

  - _____
  - _____
  - _____
  - _____

Well done on finishing this section! Complete as many of the revision sheets as you can. Date and file these away in a ring binder. Keep a record of the sheets you have completed for easy reference later. Our next chapter deals with Paper 2, Section II, the Comparative Study.

**Date completed:** _____

# Your Last Minute Revision!

### Around 5 Minutes Revision for Each Single Text Revision Sheet

● Revise your Single Text revision sheets on plot, character and theme that you made out during the year. These should be in your own revision file.

### Around 10 Minutes Revision

● Read over the tips and techniques for answering the 10-mark questions on the Single Text on page 165 and page 169.

### Around 10 Minutes Revision

● Read over the tips and techniques for answering the 30-mark question on the Single Text on page 171 and page 175. Read the tips on answering this question and the sample answers on pages 182–187.

### Check your Time Management

● Suggested timing for this section:

  ▪ **Paper 2, Section I, The Single Text** (60 marks) overall time allowance = 55 minutes (includes reading time and planning time).

# Chapter 6

## Paper 2, Sec. II – The Comparative Study

This chapter contains the following items. You should tick the boxes as you complete each.

# Introduction

There are hundreds of possible text combinations in the Comparative Study. First of all, however, ensure that your two or three texts are prescribed for the year of your exam. The various modes of comparison are explained in this chapter and there are suggested tasks on each that you can follow while revising your texts.

Some students have found this question very challenging in the past. In fact, many teachers will tell you that students' comparative answers are sometimes incoherent, unstructured and lacking in direction and focus. This chapter is designed to help you to avoid these pitfalls.

Critically important here is the need to actually make direct comparisons in your answer – several times – between two or even three texts. It is more effective and impressive if you compare texts in the same paragraphs rather than treat each text separately.

Study the sample answers closely in this chapter to see how the writers manage to compare and contrast texts successfully. However, please note that the sample answers are intended to illustrate the technique of answering this question – the texts referred to might not be prescribed for your exam. Remember too that your answer should focus on key moments in each text. There is no need to try to discuss everything in your texts – that would be an impossible task! A focused, well-planned answer will be much more effective.

## At a Glance

### What Must I Answer in Section II, the Comparative Study?

- Your task in the Comparative Study is to compare and contrast texts under different headings or modes.

- Each year, three modes of comparison are prescribed and questions on two of the modes appear on the exam paper.

- In total, there will be four comparative questions on the exam paper, two under each of the two modes of comparison on the paper.

- You are required to answer **one** of the four questions in this section.

> **The MODES OF COMPARISON for Ordinary Level are:**
> - Theme
> - Relationships
> - Social setting
> - Aspects of story – tension or climax or resolution
> - Hero/heroine/villain

- Only three of these are prescribed for any one year. Check with your teacher that you know correctly the three modes you must compare texts under for your Comparative Study. You can double check by logging onto **www.education.ie**.

## How Many Marks, How Much Time?

Paper 2, Section II, the Comparative Study is worth 70 marks.
Suggested time for planning and writing your answer is 60 minutes.

## General Advice

- You must **not** do three things!

  **1.** You may **not** use the text you have answered on in Section I, The Single Text in your comparative answer.
  **2.** You may **not** discuss two films in your answer.
  **3.** You may **not** use a text that is not on the prescribed list of texts for the year of your exam.

- When you read the word 'text' in a question, it refers to all of the different kinds of texts available for study in the comparative study, i.e. novel, play, short story, autobiography, biography, travel writing and film.

- The word 'author' in a question may refer to a novelist, playwright or film director.

- **The modes of comparison change each year.** Make sure you know which modes to study for your exam. This is especially important if you are re-sitting your exam or repeating Fifth or Sixth Year.

- The comparative question will be in two parts. Part (a) of the question asks you to discuss one text on its own. This is usually a 30-mark question. Part (b) asks you to discuss the similarities and/or differences between the text discussed in (a) with another text on your comparative course. This might be a 30-mark or 40-mark question.

- Note that while Part (b) usually asks you to discuss two texts, three texts may be studied for this section.

- **The list of texts changes each year**. Make sure your Comparative texts are prescribed for the year of your exam. This information is also available at **www.education.ie**.

- **One** of your comparative texts may be a **film**.

- Finally, you are not expected to study the comparative texts in as much detail as you would study a Single Text. **Focus on the key moments** from each text that illustrate the three modes of comparison for your exam year. A key moment may be a scene, a chapter, or a particular incident in a text. However, you may also draw points from any part of your texts, whether they are key moments or not.

> Remember, do not use your Single Text as
> one of your Comparative texts!

# RPTA

## Key Tips to Maximise your Marks

### ⊙ Key Tip 1: READ the Question Correctly

● The Comparative Study question is one that many students find challenging. To get the best possible start, it is crucial that you read the question several times until you are clear what the key instructions are.

● Sometimes, the questions in this section might seem a bit long-winded. Read the question slowly, a number of times. Break down the question and write down or underline each key instruction separately.

> If your answer is irrelevant, you will lose marks. Therefore, read each question at last three times, then underline or highlight the key terms in that question.

### ⊙ Key Tip 2: PLAN Your Answer

● Once you have a clear understanding of what's expected, start to plan your answer. Select key moments from the texts that you think will illustrate your main points most clearly. **Do not simply summarise each of the texts.**

● While planning, you may include similarities and/or differences between the two (or three) texts.

● Also, keep your focus on key moments in your plan. You are not expected to go through the entire texts. If you have learned some quotations, only use those that are relevant and help to support your points. However, be careful not to overdo it.

> Don't go off the point!
> Use a simple plan as a guide to keep you focused.

● Both Part (a) and Part (b) are worth a lot of marks! Make a plan for all questions. For the question where you have to discuss two texts, make sure your plan refers to similarities and/or differences between the texts that you are going to explore. Also, jot down a few comparative phrases that you can use.

### Key Tip 3: TIME Your Answer

Time Allowed (Paper 2):
3 Hours 20 Minutes

● The suggested time for **Section II, The Comparative Study** is approximately 60 minutes. This includes reading time and planning time.

### Key Tip 4: ANSWER the Question Asked

● Just before you begin to write your full answer, look once again at the question, then at your plan. Double check that each point in your plan is relevant to the question. Then begin. Immediately, write down the name of texts you are about to answer on, and the name of the author.

● Part (a) of the comparative question will ask you to discuss one text. There is no need to make any comparison in this question.

● Part (b) of the comparative question will ask you to discuss the similarities and/or differences between the text in Part (a) and at least one other text on your Comparative Study course. It is important that you do not write 'separate mini-essays' on each text. Practise writing answers where you **compare your texts frequently**, preferably in each paragraph!

● You should plan to write between one to one-and-a-half pages of an answer for a 30-mark question (about half a page for a 15-mark question). For a 40-mark question in which you compare two texts, write about one-and-a-half to two pages.

### Answering Tips!

● In answering the comparative question, when you start to compare and contrast texts, use phrases that show clearly the similarities and/or differences between the texts.

● For showing **SIMILARITIES**, use phrases such as:

  ▪ 'In both Text A and Text B . . .'

  ▪ 'Text A and Text B are alike in the way that they . . .'

  ▪ 'Text A and Text B explore a very similar theme.'

  ▪ 'In both Text A and Text B, the main character is admirable, inspiring, engaging, etc.'

  ▪ 'In the same way as Text A, Text B also . . .'

● Other words and phrases that are used to point to similarities include: 'Similarly', 'Once again', 'Likewise'.

● For showing **DIFFERENCES**, use phrases such as:

  ▪ 'Text B, unlike Text A, . . .'

  ▪ 'Text B explores the theme differently.'

  ▪ 'Text B's main character faces very different obstacles to those faced by the hero in Text A.'

  ▪ 'The hero in Text B is a very different person to the hero in Text A.'

  ▪ 'Text B is unique in the way it . . .'

- Other words and phrases that are used to point to differences include: 'By contrast', 'On the other hand', 'In contrast to', 'Quite the opposite occurs', 'Whereas in Text A . . . in Text B.', 'Text B differs from Text A . . .'

- If you do not compare and contrast the texts, but write separate paragraphs on each of the texts, you can expect no higher grade than a D3 for that question.

## Exam Trends

### ⦿ Exam Trends from Past Leaving Certificate English Papers – All Modes

Prescribed modes for each year shaded **green**. Modes **ticked** appeared on the exam paper.

|  | Hero/heroine/villain | Theme | Social setting | Relationships | Aspects of story |
|---|---|---|---|---|---|
| 2015 |  |  |  |  |  |
| 2014 |  |  |  |  |  |
| 2013 |  |  | ✓ |  | ✓ |
| 2012 | ✓ | ✓ |  |  |  |
| 2011 |  |  | ✓ | ✓ |  |
| 2010 | ✓ | ✓ |  |  |  |
| 2009 |  | ✓ | ✓ |  |  |
| 2008 |  |  | ✓ | ✓ |  |
| 2007 | ✓ | ✓ |  |  |  |
| 2006 |  |  | ✓ |  | ✓ |
| 2005 |  |  | ✓ | ✓ |  |
| 2004 |  | ✓ |  |  | ✓ |
| 2003 | ✓ | ✓ |  |  |  |
| 2002 |  |  | ✓ | ✓ |  |
| 2001 | ✓ |  | ✓ |  |  |

# Revising Hero/Heroine/Villain

**Suggested revision activities:**

- Identify the hero/heroine/villain in your text.

- Describe the role or part that he or she plays in the text.

- Say why you liked or disliked the hero, heroine or villain.

> ### bright Spark – a Student's Tip
>
> 'My teacher gave me good advice. She told us over and over again, not to write a summary of our texts. That advice stuck with me in the exam and I really focused on discussing the key moments while supporting my points.'
>
> *Anne*

- Describe how this person came to be a hero, heroine or villain. Note any moments where changes occurred in their character or personality through the text.

- Discuss your impression of this hero, heroine or villain. Did you find the character to be interesting, clever, kind, ruthless, devious, caring, romantic or admirable. Refer to about three key moments from the text to explain how you formed this impression.

- What similarities and/or differences can you see between the hero/heroine/villain of one text with the hero, heroine or villain of a second text on your comparative course?

- Compare the challenges/obstacles faced by the hero/heroine/villain in two of the comparative texts on your course.

- Explain how the values of the hero, heroine or villain in each text were different or similar. Refer to key moments to support your points.

- Finally, which author do you think was more successful in creating the hero, heroine or villain in your comparative texts? Explain why.

## ◉ Sample Questions on Hero, Heroine or Villain

The 30-mark question asks you to discuss one text. The 40-mark question asks you to compare this text with one, or more, other text.

● **1.** (a) Choose a hero or heroine or villain from **one** of the three texts you have studied on your comparative course. Based on the character's personality and behaviour, give reasons why you would or would not like to meet him or her. Support your answer with reference to the text. (30 marks)

(b) Choose a hero or heroine or villain from **another text** you have studied as part of your comparative course. Compare the personality and behaviour of this character with the personality and behaviour of the character you referred to in 1.(a) above. Remember to refer to both characters in the course of your answer. (40 marks)

**OR**

● **2.** (a) (i) Identify a hero or heroine or villain from one text you have studied as part of your comparative course. Give one reason why you like or dislike this character. In your answer, use one or more key moments to explain why you feel this way about the character. (15 marks)

(ii) Choose a different hero or heroine or villain from another text you have studied as part of your comparative course. Give one reason why you like or dislike this character. In your answer, use one or more key moments to explain why you feel this way about this character. (15 marks)

(b) Compare the characters you discussed above, in order to decide which of these two characters you most enjoyed studying. Remember to refer to both characters in your answer. (40 marks) (LC, OL, 2012)

# Revising Theme

**Suggested revision activities:**
● In one sentence, write down the theme of your text.
● Describe briefly what the text has to 'say' about this theme. What did you learn about the theme from the text?
● **Describe three key moments** in the text that 'show' this theme or where the theme is evident.
● Describe what happens in each key moment, then comment on how it shows/develops/ illustrates the theme clearly.

- Explain how the theme of the text affected the life of one of the characters in the text. Compare and contrast the effect the theme had on a character from a second text on your comparative course.

- Discuss any differences in the way Text A and Text B show the theme. Indicate if one is more violent, graphic, realistic, sentimental, revealing, and so on.

## Bright Spark – a Student's Tip

'My best mark in the exam was for my Comparative question Part (B) where I compared the theme of two texts. I was really pleased with this because in school it was always a tough question. Why did I score high marks? Well, I think I really made an effort to compare the two texts. In every paragraph, I mentioned similarities or differences between the two. This gave my answer a real focus. It also prevented me from writing the dreaded summaries!'

*Philip*

- Also, discuss any similarities in the way Text A and Text B show the theme.

- Explain how the theme makes your texts more entertaining, interesting or enjoyable.

## ◉ Sample Questions on Theme

**1.** (a) Identify a theme found in two of the three texts you have studied on your comparative course. In relation to **one** text you have studied, explain how you found studying this text helpful in understanding your chosen theme. (30 marks)

(b) Identify **a second text** in which you have studied the same theme. Compare relevant aspects of this text, with the one you referred to in 1. (a) above, in order to establish which text was the most helpful in developing your understanding of the theme. Remember to refer to **both texts** in your answer. (40 marks)

**OR**

**2.** (a) (i) Identify a theme from **one** text that you have studied on your comparative course and describe a key moment in which this theme is clearly evident. (15 marks)

(ii) Describe a key moment in **another text**, which you studied on your comparative course, which clearly reveals the same theme which you discussed in 2. (a)(i) above. (15 marks)

(b) Compare what you learned about your chosen theme from each of the key moments you have identified. Remember to refer to both key moments in your answer. (40 marks) (LC, OL, 2012)

# Revising Social Setting

**Suggested revision activites:**

- Describe the social setting in each text. Where did the action take place? What kind of world was it?

- Show how the social setting affected or influenced one main character in each text (in either a positive or negative way, or both). Refer to a key moment in each text in support of your points.

- Describe the features of the world of one text that you would like to visit or avoid.

- Explain why you found the social setting of one text more appealing, interesting or significant than the social setting of a second text on your comparative course.

- How were the values of people in the world of one text similar to, or different from, the values of people in a second text on your course?

## ⦿ Questions on Social Setting

**1.** (a) Choose **one** text that you have studied as part of your comparative course. Explain, with reference to at least one aspect of the social setting of that text, why you would or would not like to live in the world of that text. (30 marks)

(b) Compare the aspect(s) of social setting of the text that you referred to in (a) above with the same aspect(s) of social setting in **one or more other texts** from your comparative course. Support your answer by reference to the text that you referred to in (a) above and to at least one other text from your comparative course. (40 marks)

**OR**

**2.** 'Aspects of social setting can have a significant influence on characters' lives.'

(a) (i) Use one or more key moments, from **one** text that you have studied on your comparative course, to show that an aspect of social setting had a significant influence on the life of one character in this text. (20 marks)

(ii) Use one or more key moments, from **a different text** on your comparative course, to show that the same aspect of social setting had a significant influence on the life of one character in this text. (20 marks)

(b) Compare the way(s) in which the aspect of social setting that you identified in (a) above significantly influenced the lives of the two characters you have written about. Remember to refer to **both texts** in your answer. (30 marks) (LC, OL, 2013)

# Revising Relationships

**Suggested revision activities:**

● Describe and comment on the importance of one key relationship in each of the texts you studied on your comparative course.

● Compare one relationship in one text with one relationship in a different text. What similarities and/or differences can you see between the relationships?

● Explain how each relationship changes or develops in the text and explain why changes occurred.

● Discuss the high point/best moment and the low point/worst moment in each of the relationships. Explain how the characters responded to these two moments in the relationship.

● Discuss the relationship which you thought was more realistic, interesting, inspiring, upsetting, predictable, complicated, positive, negative or successful. **Find three pieces of evidence from each text in support of your points** and explain what this evidence tells you about the relationship.

## ◎ Questions on Relationships

1. (a) 'Relationships can be very complicated.' Describe a relationship which you have studied in one of the texts on your comparative course and explain why you found it to be complicated. (30 marks)

   (b) Choose a relationship from another text on your comparative course and explain why you found this relationship more or less complicated than the one you described. Remember to refer to both relationships in the course of your answer. (40 marks)

   **OR**

2. (a) Briefly describe a relationship from each of two of the three texts you have studied on your comparative course. (30 marks)

   (b) Explain why you think one of the relationships you described in (a) is more successful than the other. Remember to refer to both relationships in the course of your answer. (40 marks) (LC, OL, 2008)

# Revising Aspects of the Story

## Tension or Climax or Resolution

**Suggested revision activities:**

● Write a simple definition of tension, of climax and of resolution. Keep these in mind as you use key moments from your texts in support of your points.

● Describe one key moment in each text where tension, climax or resolution made an impression on you.

● Describe how the main characters were involved in the tension, climax or resolution.

● Explain how the tension, climax or resolution made the story more enjoyable, interesting, gripping or satisfying, etc.

● Explain how the author of one text created the tension, climax or resolution.

● Compare how the author of another text on your course created the tension, climax or resolution. Which author do you think was more successful? Explain why.

## ◉ Questions on Aspects of Story: Tension or Climax or Resolution

1. Choose one of the following aspects of story and answer the questions that follow:
   – Tension
   – Climax
   – Resolution

   (a) Choose any **one** of the texts that you have studied as part of your comparative course and explain how any one of the above aspects of story added to your enjoyment of this text. (30 marks)

   (b) Compare the way(s) the same aspect of story added to your enjoyment of **one or more other texts** from your comparative course. Support your answer by reference to the text that you referred to in (a) above and to at least one other text from your comparative course. (40 marks)

**OR**

2. (a) (i) Use one or more key moments to demonstrate where tension or climax or resolution is revealed in **one** text from your comparative course. (20 marks)

   (ii) Use one or more key moments to demonstrate where the same aspect of story (tension or climax or resolution) is revealed in **another text** from your comparative course. (20 marks)

   (b) Compare the impact your chosen aspect of the story made on you in each of your chosen texts. Remember to refer to **both texts** in your answer. (40 marks)
   (LC, OL, 2013)

## ◎ Answering Tips!

● If Part (a) of the question asks you to explore one text, then do just that. There is no need to make comparisons in this question. Instead, you focus on one text.

● Begin by naming your text and its author. Then make a clear statement indicating the overall viewpoint you are going to take in this answer.

● The strength of your answer will depend on the evidence you can include to illustrate, explain or support your points. Focus on key moments. Do not write a summary of the text.

● For Part (b), where instructed, make comparisons between the texts in each paragraph. Clear comparisons earn higher marks. Use the appropriate phrases to show similarities and/or differences.

● You could write down a few of these phrases onto your exam paper/answer booklet beside the question. This will remind you to use them in your answer.

> **HINT** Don't just describe a key moment. Comment on it and say what it shows about the mode you are discussing.

● Make sure you understand and can discuss the main differences between two texts on your course in relation to the three modes of comparison for the year of your exam.

● Write down the three modes of comparison here:

**Year of my Exam: 20___**

Modes of Comparison for Exam:

- Mode 1 _____
- Mode 2 _____
- Mode 3 _____

● You know you have to focus on the key moments of each text in your answer. A key moment might be a chapter, a scene, a particular incident, or even a line of dialogue. Key moments should be significant and show you something about the text's theme, hero, setting and so on. However, you can still refer to any part of a text in support of your points.

# Sample Answers

**Note!** The sample answers below are provided for illustrative purposes only. They show you how to **plan** your answer, **structure** your points and **use evidence** from a text in support of each point.

> Remember RPTA that you used for Paper 1.
> Read the question carefully. Plan your answer.
> Know your Time allowance. Double check that you are about to Answer the question that is asked.

## 2007: Theme

● **1.** (a) Describe how your chosen theme is presented in **one** of the texts. (30 marks)

(b) Compare the way in which the same theme is presented in a **second text** with the way it has been presented in the text in (a) above. To begin your answer use one of the following statements:

- 'I thought the theme in my first text was more powerful/less powerful than the theme in my second text because . . .'

- 'I enjoyed the theme of one text more than the other because . . .'

## ◉ Student's Answer Plan *(My Left Foot)*

**1. (a) Name text, author and theme; describe how theme is presented.**

● Introduction – state chosen theme.

● Paragraph 2 – focus on one text – cerebral palsy – Christy Brown – very dependent on others.

● Paragraph 3 – different to his other brothers and sisters.

● Paragraph 4 – outside the home, neighbours call him a 'dunce'.

● Paragraph 5 – art gallery – success as a painter.

● Conclusion – positive and negative aspects of living with a disability.

**Sample Answer to 1. (a)**

*Text: My Left Foot*

*Director:* Jim Sheridan

*Chosen theme:* Different Lives

One of the key themes that I studied in the film *My Left Foot*, directed by Jim Sheridan, was the theme of different lives. Through the character of Christy Brown, Jim Sheridan presents an interesting, biographical account of how a disability affects the way Christy Brown lives his life. It is a fascinating look at the highs and lows of coping with and finally overcoming a disability. In addition, the film also presents a valuable insight into how people in the community react to a person who is seen to be 'different'.

In the film, the central character Christy Brown is born with cerebral palsy. This condition means that Christy has little power in his limbs. As a child, it meant he was extremely dependent on the care of others who would feed him and carry him up the narrow stairway of his home in Dublin. In several scenes, we see his mother feed him even when he is a boy of around eight or nine. His mother also has to carry him up the stairs. The physical burden of lifting a young boy up a flight of stairs symbolises the huge demands placed on Mrs Brown in trying to provide for Christy.

The director explores the theme of disability and how it affects Christy's life in the home. In several scenes, we see Christy crouch beneath the stairs as his brothers and sisters sit around the kitchen table at breakfast and then leave him behind as they walk off to school. Christy is different and at times like this, it pains him that he cannot simply be like the others.

Out on the street we see that Christy faces obstacles too. His father has to put together the 'Chariot', a make-shift wheelchair that means the family can at least take Christy outside for some air. He plays in goal during a soccer match and although his brothers try to include him in teenage games of spin-the-bottle, Christy is still 'different' and branded a cripple. His neighbours and even some of his own family find it hard to understand this difference. When his mother is admitted to hospital to have another baby, a neighbour tries to teach Christy the alphabet and finally concludes that D is for dunce. He is also called a 'poor unfortunate gobshite'. His father also sees Christy as being 'different' or less able. He is convinced that Christy would not know what a quarter of a quarter is, saying 'shur what would he know'. This is ironic since he himself has a problem working out the answer and finally dismisses it as a stupid question.

---

*Theme is identified in first paragraph.*

*Name text and author.*

*Examples of Christy's dependencies*

*Story is commented on, not just summarised.*

*Text highlights how everyday activities have to be approached differently.*

*Appropriate quotation.*

Positive
presentation of
the theme.

Personal
response.

The theme of living differently is explored further when the film tells the story of Christy's adult life. Christy has perfected the use of his left foot for writing and painting, and is rewarded with an exhibition of his paintings. Some enlightened adults see beyond Christy's disability and can see his potential, first as a painter, then as a writer. Peter remarks at the art gallery that Christy is not a great cripple painter but a great painter. This was one of my favourite moments in the film where I thought the director presented a very positive outlook on people with disability. I enjoyed the way the film suggested that Christy was an able, rather than a disabled person.

Nonetheless, the film does not present a romanticised version of Christy's 'difference'. Scenes showing Christy's struggle with language and with love – 'Fuck platonic love' – and his tendency to lose himself in alcohol at moments of deep depression show the darker side of Christy's life. Overall, the film presents a realistic picture of the highs and lows of living with a disability.

Brief
conclusion
referring
back to the
question.

## Answering Techniques

● Name the text, the author and where required, the chosen theme.

● Introduce your answer. Make a general statement about the area that you are going to explore in your answer.

● How a text presents a theme simply means what the text has to say about the theme, what it shows about the theme.

● Briefly introduce the character under discussion.

● Identify some key moments/scenes/chapters where the theme was explored. Make a comment on the scene: what does it show?

● Choose another scene/moment where the theme is explored further. Briefly say what happened in the scene, then explain how it develops the theme that you have chosen.

● Where appropriate, you can make a personal response to a particularly moving or significant scene/key moment. However, your personal comments must be relevant to the question.

● Your conclusion should refer back to the key terms of the question.

## ◉ Student's Answer Plan
### (The Curious Incident of the Dog in the Night-time)

**1. (b) Name text, author and theme; describe how theme is presented.**

● Introduction – state chosen theme.

● Paragraph 1 – statement about text that is more powerful in presenting a different way of living.

● Paragraph 2 – Christopher's eccentric behaviour – fascinating and disturbing, deals with many things on his own. Contrast this with Christy (My Left Foot), often his family are there for him.

● Paragraph 3 – nasty name-calling – 'spazzer' – cruel reaction of others, Christopher is more hurt than Christy, a 'dunce/gobshite'.

● Paragraph 4 – many behavioural problems, but little help from his mother; contrast with Christy's mother who offers huge emotional support to Christy.

● Paragraph 5 – Christopher's gift with numbers is more amazing to me than Christy's gift with paint and words.

● Conclusion – restate overall viewpoint.

### Sample Answer to I.(b)

> *Second text and author identified.*

> *This is the prompt included in the question.*

> *Only write out title in full at the beginning of the answer.*

The theme of different lives is also explored in my second text, *The Curious Incident of the Dog in the Night-time*, written by Mark Haddon. In this novel, the central character Christopher Boone has Asperger's Syndrome. This is a mild form of autism and it affects many aspects of Christopher's life. I thought the theme of different lives in my first text, *My Left Foot* (MLF) was less powerful than the same theme in my second text, *The Curious Incident of the Dog in the Night-time* (CID) for several reasons.

Firstly, the central character of the novel, Christopher Boone is 15 years old and attending school. I have never met a person with this syndrome before and the graphic pictures of how it made Christopher's life so different were fascinating and disturbing to me. While Christy Brown's struggle to express himself was indeed interesting, I was completely fascinated and at times upset by the eccentric behaviour of Christopher in CID. When he feels threatened, for example, he makes 'the noise that father calls groaning'. Christopher says that when too much information is coming into his head, that 'groaning' is his way of blocking out the world. Christopher sometimes likes to be alone and withdraw himself away from the world. Christy in MLF can sometimes do this too, lying in bed under the covers. However, in CID, when Christopher wants to be on his own, he gets 'into the airing cupboard in the bathroom and slides in beside the boiler' and pulls the door closed behind him where he can 'sit and think for hours' to make himself feel 'calm'. By contrast, in Christy Brown's house there was always someone there to turn to, to share a problem with. Sometimes, it seemed to me that Christopher was fighting his condition on his own. This is what made his situation seem more absorbing to me than Christy's.

ENGLISH EXTRA!

At school, Christopher has to listen to name-calling because he is different. One boy at school, Terry, 'said I would only ever get a job collecting supermarket trolleys or cleaning out donkey shit at an animal sanctuary.' The boys also refer to him as a 'spazzer'. This, to me, is far more hurtful than the scene where Christy's neighbour calls him a 'gobshite'. It shows how your peers can be so cruel to you if your life is different in any way. I think Christopher is very sensitive to what others think unlike Christy Brown who is more thick-skinned. For example, in school when Siobhan speaks to the class about the way other boys call names, Christopher is quick to recall 'sometimes the children from the school down the road see us in the street when we're getting off the bus and they shout, 'Special Needs! Special Needs!' This powerfully captures the thoughtless teasing and bullying that is directed against those who are seen to be 'different'. I think CID presented this aspect more powerfully than MLF.

Like Christy Brown, who repeatedly smashes his head against a wall, and tears a tablecloth off a restaurant table in rage, Christopher Boone also has numerous behavioural problems. He makes a list of his unusual behaviour and includes points such as: 'Not talking to people for a long time, screaming when I am angry or confused, smashing things when I am angry or confused, groaning, not eating other food if different sorts of food are touching each other.'

He also does not like touching other people and even when he meets his mother after an epic journey to London, he refuses to take her hand when she outstretches hers to his in a gesture of love and friendship. This is a powerful and very sad moment where you are willing him to embrace his mother in reconciliation. This is in complete contrast to Christy Brown who at least can rely on the unconditional love of his mother who is always there for him. Mrs Brown knows Christy even more than he knows himself sometimes, and her anxiety that Christy's voice has 'too much hope in it' reveals how aware she is of her son's struggle in life.

Finally, I think Christopher Boone's unique abilities were presented in a more powerful way than Christy's gift with words. Christopher has a very special gift for maths. He is the first person to do an A level from his school. For example, he thinks 251 x 864 is 'a really easy sum'. To me, that is just remarkable. He also has an incredible memory; for example, he can memorise the exact colour patterns on each of 19 different cows he sees in a field. He can also remember all of the advertisements in the underground railway station. This is incredibly different to what I would usually think of as having a special gift or ability. I was more impressed with this gift than with Christy's gift for painting and writing which we hear more of in the media on a regular basis.

**Side annotations:**

Focus is kept firmly on the theme of 'difference'.

Useful and clear examples

Appropriate quotation.

Appropriate quotations highlights theme of 'difference'.

Writer comments on the scene.

Concise but apt quotation is effective.

Signal that answer is moving towards a conclusion.

> While both the film MLF and the novel CID presented an interesting story of people living a life that is 'different' to the norm, I think the novel presented a more gripping and at times heart-rending insight into the difficulties and the loneliness that sometimes comes with living a different life.

Brief conclusion restates writer's opinion.

### Answering Techniques

- Name the second text and the author.

- You may use abbreviations for the texts after first writing their titles out in full.

- Make comparisons from the very beginning.

- Comparison means you can say what is similar about the texts and/or what is different about the texts.

- For each paragraph, write down your key point. Say how it applies to one text. Then say how it is shown in a second text. Finally, say which text shows your point more powerfully and why.

- Use phrases such as 'unlike', 'while', 'in both' as you compare the two texts. This will help to draw the reader's attention to a comparative point.

- You should refer to key moments, scenes, events, situations or incidents in the text.

- You may also quote occasionally from the texts.

- Your conclusion should refer back to the key terms of the question.

# Key Exam Tips

## 🔑 Key Exam Tips and Techniques for the Comparative Study

- On your exam paper, write down your time allowance for this question beside the actual question.

- Read the question, at least twice. After your first reading, underline the key instructions.

- Once you understand clearly what the question is instructing you to do, you must plan your answer. This need only take a few minutes, but it is time very well spent.

- Write about one to one-and-a-half pages to answer a 20 or 30-mark question.

- Write about one-and-a-half to two pages to answer a 30 or 40-mark question.

- In writing your answer, remain focused on following the instructions. Do not drift off the point.

- Remember only two of the prescribed three modes will appear on the exam paper. Two questions will be given on each of the two modes, and you answer all parts of these questions.

- Plan your answer, especially important for the question where you must compare two texts.

- Identify the key moments in each text that will best support your answer.

- The 'easiest' mistake to make is to summarise both texts. Make sure you do not fall into this 'trap'. You must briefly describe, then comment on, key moments.

- Don't be afraid of making a personal response – but you must make reference back to the text to ensure you earn higher marks.

> You cannot use a Single Text that you have already answered as part of your Comparative Study.

## ◉ Record of What I Have Learned Revising for the Comparative Study

### Main Things to Prepare for

- **Answering the questions on hero, heroine or villain**

  - _____
  - _____
  - _____
  - _____

- **Answering the questions on theme**

  - _____
  - _____
  - _____
  - _____

- **Answering the questions on relationships**

  - _____
  - _____
  - _____
  - _____

- **Answering the questions on social setting**

  - _____
  - _____
  - _____
  - _____

- **Answering the questions on aspects of story**

  - _____
  - _____
  - _____
  - _____

Well done on completing this section! Complete as many of the revision activities as you can. Date and file your notes away into a ring binder.

**Date completed:** _____

# Your Last Minute Revision

## Around 45 Minutes Revision for Each Comparative Text: Three Modes

Revise each Comparative Text, focusing only on the three modes of comparison.
Take 15 minutes on each mode for each text.

## Around 10 Minutes

● Read over the tips and techniques for answering on the Comparative Texts.

## Around 5 Minutes
## Check Your Time Management

● Paper 2, Section II the Comparative Study (70 marks) overall time allowance =
approximately 60 minutes (includes reading time and planning time).

# Chapter 7

## Paper 2, Sec. III – Poetry

This chapter contains the following sections. You should tick the boxes as you complete each.

- ● Introduction ☐
- ● The Unseen Poem ☐
- ● Prescribed Poetry ☐
- ● Sample Answers to Prescribed Poetry ☐
- ● Key Exam Tips ☐
- ● Your Last Minute Revision! ☐

# Introduction

The poetry section is challenging, but this chapter will help you to effectively meet that challenge. You need the confidence to believe in your own interpretation in addition to the writing skills to shape your response into an interesting, thoughtful and insightful answer.

Read the Unseen Poem slowly and several times and pay attention to its language, imagery and rhythm. There are lots of tips in the following pages to help you address the Unseen Poem and a Study Card on some key terms, which you might find useful in planning your response.

You are encouraged to give a personal response in the poetry section, so your language should not always be distant or too academic. Study the kind of questions to expect in this chapter and practise writing sample answers. Over time, this will increase your confidence in writing interesting answers to the Prescribed Poems.

 **At a Glance**

### What Must I Answer in the Poetry Section?

● You must answer the questions on the Unseen Poem **and** the questions on **one** of the Prescribed Poems.

● Remember, only one Unseen Poem will be printed on the exam paper, so you have no choice with this question. However, four Prescribed Poems will be printed on the exam paper and you answer the questions on only one of these.

### How Many Marks, How Much Time?

Paper 2, Section III, Poetry is worth 70 marks: 20 marks for answering the questions on one Unseen Poem. The remaining 50 marks are for answering the questions on one of the Prescribed Poems, which will be printed on the exam paper.

● The suggested time for planning and writing your answer is 65 minutes. (15 minutes approximately on the Unseen Poem and about 50 minutes on the Prescribed Poem.)

# The Unseen Poem

### Unseen Poem (20 marks) – 15 minutes

- Answer all of the questions on the Unseen Poem. Expect to see two questions, each worth 10 marks.

- Read the brief introduction to the poem (where it is given). Read the poem at least three times before answering. Sometimes, the introduction explains the context of the poem, or the background to the poem. This can help you to understand the general gist of a poem, i.e. what it is about. For example, in 2009, the poem 'Sentimental Moment' appeared on the exam paper. The introduction read: 'In this poem, the writer Robert Hershon tells of a moment in a restaurant with his adult son.'

- Think about the poem's **title**. A title usually points towards a key idea or a key moment in a poem.

- At times, you might see a small asterisk, like this *, beside a word in a poem. This means there is a brief note explaining the word. Make sure you read it.

- Do not just read the poem as you would read a newspaper article. Read the words carefully, look out for patterns in the use of words; look out for the use of imagery (similes and metaphors).

> ### Bright Spark – a Student's Tip
> 'I did really well in my Unseen Poem. I remember that I didn't just summarise the poem in my own words. I tried to describe how the poet used language in the poem to make it interesting and effective.'
>
> *Tom*

- Try to 'hear' the poem – listen for sounds made by alliteration, assonance and onomatopoeia.

- Try to get a feel for the overall atmosphere of the poem or mood of the poet. Is it one of anger, happiness, pride, sorrow and so on?

- Make sure you read each question very carefully. Underline the key instruction. This should help you to avoid the quite common pitfall of students rambling on and on about the poem without actually answering the question at all!

- You are encouraged to respond in a personal way to the Unseen Poem.

- However, you may also use poetic terms such as alliteration, imagery, simile and so on where it helps you to make your point more clearly. See the Study Card No. 22 on page 220 for notes on terms that might be helpful to you while answering on an Unseen Poem.

- The time allowance is about 15 minutes. Long answers are not expected here. For each 10-mark question, around 10 lines are adequate, no more than half an A4 page.

## What Kind of Questions to Expect

Here are some of the questions on the Unseen Poem from past exam papers:

**1. Questions asking for your impression of a place, a person, or a relationship in a poem** (see examples from exam papers in 2012, 2010, 2009, 2005 and 2002).

## Answering Tips!

- When you answer, identify the words and phrases that give you this impression and explain your choice. In a 10-mark question, only 4 marks would go for writing your impression – most marks (6) go for explaining how you got this impression, so always refer to the language in the poem to explain your point.

- When commenting on the world of a poem, begin with a general statement about that world. The world in the poem could be a very poor, demanding, scary, threatening, loving or carefree place. Then select some words, images or phrases from the poem and explain how they give you that impression.

**Example**

> I think Terry Street is a tense, unfriendly and possibly poor neighbourhood. The writer seems relieved that his neighbours are moving out. The mischievous son, in particular, will not be missed, the writer being 'glad' to see him 'removed'. It gives me the impression that the writer did not get on particularly well with his neighbours. I do not think he had much time for the 'whistling youths' dressed in 'US Army battle-jackets'. However, the writer holds no grudge against them and at the end of the poem wishes them well, wishes them 'grass'. This is an unusual phrase. It shows clearly just how grey Terry Street is, a place of concrete yards without the softness, colour nor beauty of gardens. That hard, grey physical landscape is a symbol of the cold, impersonal relationship between the writer and 'that man'. I noticed that the poet decided not to use dialogue in the poem. This is appropriate because it reinforces my impression that Terry Street was not a pleasant or friendly world in which to live. (2006, Q1)

## 2. Questions asking you to comment on a line or lines in a poem
(see examples from 2010, 2007, 2005, 2004 and 2003.)

### ◉ Answering Tips!

● You may be asked:

- To explain a line or lines.

- To select your favourite lines.

- To choose lines that show the poet's or others feelings.

- To select lines that you think are most effective in the poem.

When you select a line or lines, do not just give a general, vague reason to support your point. Try to give precise reasons why you chose certain lines. For example, *'The lines that capture the lover's feelings are lines 8 and 9. These are good and clear lines'*, is just too vague (2003, Q2). It says very little. A better way to respond might be: *'Lines 8 and 9 capture the lover's feelings very effectively. The image of the poet wanting to kiss "each individual hair of your head" shows very clearly his desire for his lover. He seems to be passionately in love with her.'* In other words, explain clearly why you have selected certain lines in the poem.

## 3. Questions asking you to create a different title for a poem
(see examples from 2009).

### ◉ Answering Tips!

Refer closely to the text of the poem. You may select another word or words from the poem to create a new title. Or, you could create a title based on your own reading of the poem. Explain why you think your title is a good/interesting/appropriate one.

## 4. Questions asking you to choose descriptions in a poem or sections in a poem that appeal to you (see example from 2008).

### ◉ Answering Tips!

Descriptions in a poem may appeal to readers for many different reasons. Write down the description from the poem, then say why it is appealing. Refer to the poet's choice of words. For example, do you like the way the poet uses images or sounds in the poem to make it interesting, enjoyable or revealing? A description may also appeal to you because it brings back happy memories, reminds you of a special place or person, or perhaps because it creates a very exciting or desirable image of that place/person in your mind.

> **HINT** In answering any Unseen Poem question, it is important that you support your points by close reference to the text of the poem. Refer to the poem's language and imagery.

## 5. Questions asking you to explain a key idea in a poem
(see examples from 2013, 2012, 2008, 2006 and 2001).

### ◯ Answering Tips!

● To explain a key idea in the poem, you certainly can give your own viewpoints based on a personal reading. However, you must read the poem very closely and then select words/phrase/images that the poet uses to convey the poem's key idea.

● Write down these words/phrases, then explain how they get across the poem's main idea or message.

## 6. Questions asking for your overall impression of feelings about a poem
(see examples from 2011, 2006, 2003 and 2001).

### ◯ Answering Tips!

● Firstly, write down what your overall impression is: *Overall, I think this poem is very dramatic/sad/funny* and so on. Then explain why you think this.

**Example**

> I think it is a sad poem because it describes the decline of a city and shows how 'choked' and 'churned' it has become. Several images give me the impression that the city regrets human interference in its life. For example, in line 8 the city tells us 'They put murder into my head' and in line 12 the city regrets that people have 'turned my heart to stone'. These phrases create a sad, sorrowful atmosphere in the poem. In the final stanza, the city's helpless and hopeless cry for some relief is quite sad because I think the city knows itself that it will never again 'grow like wheat from the grain'. This simile is very powerful in showing the city's yearning for a better life.
>
> I also got the impression that this poem was a sad one because the poet, Gareth Owen, used personification so the city speaks of its ill-treatment as if it were a human being. For example, the city tells us: 'My brain is stiff with concrete/My limbs are rods of steel'. In addition, the fact that the speaker in the poem is the city means that the heartache of the city is told to us in a very intimate and personal way. This all helps to create my impression of a sad poem. (2006, Q1)

**7. Questions asking what you like or dislike about a poem**
    (see examples from 2002).

### ◉ Answering Tips!

When saying what you like about a poem you could focus on any one of several areas:

- The subject/theme of the poem. Perhaps you found that the main message of the poem was interesting, or made you think about the theme in a new or different way. Perhaps the poem's main idea had never occurred to you before. Perhaps you liked how unusual or original the main idea was.

- You could say that you liked the poem because of how well it was written. Give examples of interesting word choice, use of imagery, sound effects, and so on.

- You could say that you liked the poem because you found it amusing, unusual or creative.

- You could say you liked the poem because it connected with you in a personal way. Perhaps it shed light on some aspect of your own life? Perhaps the poem's setting is one with which you are familiar. Or, perhaps it painted a world you had never thought of before.

# Prescribed Poetry

**Prescribed Poetry (50 marks) – 50 minutes**

Answer the questions on one of the Prescribed Poems. Expect four poems to appear in this section.

- Each of these four poems will be printed, usually in full, on the exam paper.

> Two of the Prescribed Poems are taken from the list of poems only studied by Ordinary Level students. The other two poems are taken from the list of poems common to Ordinary and Higher Level students.

- In your answer, try to show your understanding of the poem.

- Avoid writing very short answers that simply make a brief statement, without reference or support, and that do not engage with the poem in any real detail at all.

- Every time you make a key point, use the poem – its content and its language – to support your views.

However, just because the poem is printed on the paper, do not be tempted to write down huge chunks of the poem – there is little to be gained from this. Better to quote a few phrases, perhaps a line or two from different sections of the poem that are relevant to the point you are making.

## Questions 1(i), 1(ii) and 1(iii) (30 marks)

###  What Kind of Questions to Expect

> You must answer each of the questions 1(i), 1(ii) and 1(iii).

The first set of questions, 1(i), 1(ii) and 1(iii), usually ask you questions directly linked with the text of the poem itself. Typical questions like this would include:

- From your reading of this poem do you think the father and daughter have a good relationship? Explain your answer.

- Do you think this is a sad or funny poem or both? Explain your answer.

- What details in stanzas 1 and 2 of this poem create the sense of early morning in Finglas? Explain your answer.

- According to Yeats, what qualities do the swans at Coole Park possess? Explain your answer.

- Which is your favourite stanza in the poem? Explain why you like it.

- Do you think this poem is serious or humorous or both? Explain your answer with reference to the poem.

- Choose one phrase or line from the poem that you find particularly appealing. Explain your choice.

- What impression of the poet, Elizabeth Bishop, do you get from reading the poem?

You can see that these questions expect you to give your opinion and also to *explain* your opinions. You must give reasons for them. These questions expect a close reading of the poem. You must refer back to the words and phrases in the poem and try to explain your viewpoint.

It is really important that you do this because **most of the marks are awarded for explaining your answer**. 1(i), 1(ii) and 1(iii) are worth 10 marks each. Essentially, 4 marks out of 10 would go for writing your point of view. But the other 6 marks out of 10 would go for explaining why you *have* that point of view. If you were to leave out the 'why' part of each answer, you would lose up to 18 marks out of 30 for questions 1(i), 1(ii) and 1(iii).

When discussing words, phrases and lines from the poem, you might find some of the terms described in Study Card No. 22 on the next page useful and helpful in making your points more clearly.

## Study Card No. 22: Poetic Terms

- **Alliteration**

  - Alliteration is the repetition of identical consonant sounds in words.

  - Poets may use this technique to connect key words in a poem. It can also produce a pleasing effect to the ear when the line is read aloud.
    'Tears in the kitchen, telephone-calls
    To school from your freedom-loving father'
    *('For Heidi with Blue Hair' by Fleur Adcock)*

- **Assonance**

  - Assonance is another sound device. It occurs where a writer uses similar vowel sounds in words.
    'shapes like full-blown roses
    Stained and lost through age'
    *('The Fish' by Elizabeth Bishop)*

- **Diction**

  - Diction refers to the type of words used in a poem. Some poems may include many ordinary, everyday words. Other poems may include more formal or technical words.

  - When you look at the poet's choice of words, try to suggest why these words were used. For example, why ordinary words? Or, why scholarly words? Or, why old-fashioned words?

  - Many modern poets use conversational language which is ideal in poems where the writer is sharing a personal story with the reader. It creates a personal, intimate tone between the writer and the reader and gives a kind of chatty, sometimes intimate effect to the poem.

- **Emotive Language**

  - Emotive language is used to show an emotional reaction to a poem's subject. It can also be used to create an emotional response in you, the reader.
    'He collapsed beside his carpet-slippers
    Without a murmur, shot through the head
    By a shivering boy who wandered in
    Before they could turn the television down.'
    *('Wounds' by Michael Longley)*

- **Irony**

  - Irony is where words say one thing but may also be read to mean the very opposite.

● **Metaphor**

- A metaphor is a word or phrase that shows a likeness between two things that usually would not be considered to have any similarity.
  'The light of her stable-lamp was a star'
  (*'A Christmas Childhood' by Patrick Kavanagh*)

● **Onomatopoeia**

- Onomatopoeia is a word that, when spoken aloud, imitates the sound made. Examples include *hiss, sizzle, cuckoo, pop* and *splash.*
- Poets may use onomatopoeia so their poems appeal to our senses. It can also add an element of fun and playfulness to some poems.

● **Persona**

- The speaker or voice of the poem is its persona. Usually, the persona is the poet. However, this is not always the case. In the first example below, the poet is Yeats, but the speaker is the airman Robert Gregory. In the second example, John Montague is the poet and the speaker.
  'I know that I shall meet my fate
  Somewhere among the clouds above.'
  (*'An Irish Airman Foresees his Death' by W.B. Yeats*)

  'My father, the least happy
  Man I have known.'
  (*'The Cage' by John Montague*)

● **Personification**

- Personification is a type of metaphor where objects are given human characteristics.
  'There were stars in the morning east
  And they danced to his music'
  (*'A Christmas Childhood' by Patrick Kavanagh*)

● **Rhyme**

- End-rhyme occurs where the final word of one line of poetry rhymes with the final word of another line.
  'Delight men's eyes when I awake some day
  To find they have flown away?'
  (*'The Wild Swans at Coole' by W.B. Yeats*)

- **Simile**
  - A simile is an imaginative comparison between two things or actions using like, as or than.

    '
    . . . heart
    Breaks loose and rolls down like a stone.'
    (*'After the Titanic' by Derek Mahon*)

- **Symbol**
  - A symbol is a type of image where a word also stands for something other than itself. For example, the Irish flag is a symbol for the country of Ireland. The dove represents peace. The heart is a symbol of love.

- **Theme**
  - The theme is the central idea of a poem. It usually shows the poet's attitude towards a subject, place or person.

 **Questions 2(i), 2(ii) and 2(iii) (20 marks)**

### What Kind of Questions to Expect

Many of the tasks in Question 2 ask for an imaginative or creative response by suggesting, for example, that you are a character in the poem, or that you live in the setting of the poem, and so on.

> You only answer one of the questions 2(i), 2(ii) or 2(iii).
> Do not waste time answering all three. Put your time into
> writing one full answer for 20 marks (write at least 20 lines).

You answer **one** question only here. Each part is worth 20 marks. Expect a wide range of questions, some linked directly with the poem, others more loosely based on the text and requiring a more creative and imaginative response. Examples include the following:

- You have been asked to make a short video to accompany a reading of this poem on YouTube. Describe the images, colours, music, sound effects, etc. that you would use as a background to the reading and explain your choices based on your knowledge of the poem. In your answer you may choose to refer to the extract provided or to the poem as a whole. (2013, Poem C, Q.2 (iii) )

- Imagine you are the young Seamus Heaney. Write a diary entry about the day the constable called. Your diary entry should be based on your reading of the poem. (2012, Poem A, Q2 (iii) )

- In which one of the following collections of poetry do you feel this poem best belongs?
    - A collection of poems about nature.
    - A collection of poems about beauty.
    - A collection of poems about life.
- Give reasons for your choice with reference to the poem. (2012, Poem B, Q.2 (iii) )
- Did the language used by the poet in this poem appeal to you? Explain your answer with reference to the poem. (2011, Poem B, Q.2 (i) )
- Imagine Heidi, now 20 years older, finds a photograph of herself as a teenager with blue hair. Write a piece beginning with one of the following statements:
    - I can't believe I did such a thing.
    - I'm so glad I did that. (2010, Poem A, Q2 [ii])
- Imagine that Paula Meehan's father kept a diary. Write a diary entry in which he expresses his thoughts and feelings about feeding the birds at dawn. (2010, Poem B, Q2 [i])
- You decide to create a short video to capture the atmosphere of this poem. Describe how you might use location, lighting, soundtrack, music, etc. to communicate this. (2010, Poem B, Q2 [ii])
- Based on this poem write an article for a travel magazine in which you encourage tourists to visit Coole Park. (2010, Poem D, Q2 [i])
- While at first glance you might think you can 'write anything' to these types of questions, be careful. While you are given the freedom to be original and creative, your answer should also refer back to the text of the poem.

> ### Examiner's Tip!
> For any questions that ask you to write a diary or a newspaper report or create a short video, make sure you use details from the poem in your answer.

# Sample Answers

## to Prescribed Poetry

Study the sample answer on page 224. If you were writing the diary of Paula Meehan's father (2010, Poem B, Q2 [i]) in which he expresses his feelings about feeding the birds, you should use the text of the poem as a resource. The question states that the diary must 'express his thoughts and feelings about feeding the birds at dawn'.

**2010: Poem B, Question 2 (i)**

Imagine that Paula Meehan's father kept a diary. Write a diary entry in which he expresses his thoughts and feelings about feeding the birds at dawn.

> Remember **RPTA** that you used for Paper 1.
> **R**ead the question carefully.
> **P**lan your answer.
> Know your **T**ime allowance.
> **A**nswer the question that is asked.

## ◎ Student's Answer Plan

**Focus on thoughts/feelings on feeding birds, dawn; also, use details in poem**

- Paragraph 1 – wake up early – hear sounds first thoughts are of birds.

- Paragraph 2 – out in back yard, ready for birds; use poem for ideas, e.g. the cold, frosty morning.

- Paragraph 3 – concentrate on feeding the birds and my feelings and thoughts.

**Sample Answer**

24 November

Good morning Diary,

I awoke a little earlier than usual today. I lay in bed for over an hour, wondering how the birds survived last night's frost. Getting dressed, I heard Joe the milkman, delivering the milk at my gate. On time as usual. Once up, I cleaned out the fireplace and made a cup of hot tea and had a piece of toast for breakfast. It was a lovely bright morning and I found my self humming an old song as I broke up a few slices of bread for the birds. Ah the birds, my birds, where would I be without them.

I unlocked the back door and stepped into the garden. I was glad I was wearing a coat for a cold autumn breeze blew in from the east. It was quiet at first. I could hear the early bus pull away from O'Reilly's corner down the road. I knew my birds would not be long now. And then they came, in their hundreds. I loved the various colours of their wings, the peculiar ways different birds hopped and flitted across the yard. And then their chatter and song. It was the best part of my day.

The crows are always first to arrive, but the tits and starlings are never far behind. It is a wonderful feeling to share these few precious moments with the birds. It does my heart good. I always love that moment when I gather a last fistful of crumbs and hold out both arms fully, before tossing the last of the precious crumbs into the air. The excitement of the birds at feeding time, and my own joy, is something that I will never forget.

Dad

**Answering Techniques**
- 'Bottles chinked on the doorstep' – stanza 1.
- 'hum a snatch of a tune' – stanza 2.
- 'Autumn was nearly done, the first frost whitened the slates of the estate' – stanza 3.
- 'They came then: birds of every size, shape, colour' – stanza 4.
- 'when my father threw up his hands and tossed the crumbs to the air' – stanza 5.

Another question that may appear is one which asks if you think the poem's title is a good one or not. Obviously, you begin by making your opening statement, saying that you think it is or is not a good title. But you must read the poem very closely and focus in on words and phrases which help to explain why you think the title is effective or not. An example is shown below.

**Sample Question**
From your understanding of the poem, do you think 'Wounds' is a good title for it? Explain your answer. ('Wounds' by Michael Longley)

## ◎ Student's Answer Plan – Spider Diagram Plan

The points in a spider diagram (spidergram) might look like this:

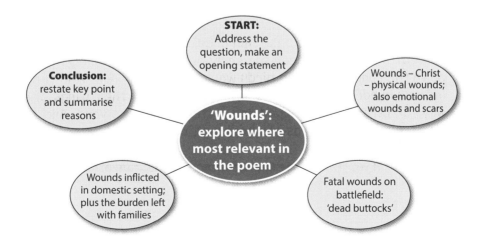

## Sample Answer

Michael Longley has chosen the title 'Wounds' for this poem. I think this is a very appropriate title for several reasons.

Immediately, this title makes me think of the suffering over many hundreds of years, back even to the time of Christ and his torture and crucifixion. The wounds in Longley's poem include horrific physical wounds, the wounds of misunderstanding and the emotional wounds and scars that have to be borne by families who have lost loved ones.

The title is at first linked with two pictures from the memory of the poet's father, secrets that are to be shared with us. The father's words, which recall the terrible scenes at the Somme, where hundreds of young men were slaughtered, are 'words/Of admiration and bewilderment'. The landscape of 'dead buttocks' is a disturbing image of the fatal wounds inflicted on young soldiers. For those who survive the battlefield, the 'lucky' ones who return home with lost limbs and shellshock, there are always 'badges' and 'medals like rainbows'. The title 'Wounds' certainly reflects the harrowing experience of soldiers in battle for 'King and Country'.

The wounds inflicted on civilians are equally horrific. Longley paints graphic and once again disturbing pictures of the dead and the moment of their dying. His language captures the injustice and brutality of violence in a domestic setting of 'carpet slippers' and 'supper dishes'. The savagery of the attack on the bus conductor, 'shot though the head' leaves his devastated wife in emotional turmoil. She too has to bear the emotional wounds of losing her loved one for many years to come.

'Wounds' is perhaps the only title this poem could have. Longley paints a gruesome picture of suffering on the battlefield and even more disturbingly, in a domestic setting. In addition, he is mindful of the survivors, those left behind with the emotional wounds – the young children left with no father, and the 'bewildered' wife left without her husband.

## Answering Techniques

- Begin with a brief introduction.
- Explore briefly what the title 'says' to you.
- Focus on the title – 'Wounds' – explore different types of wounds in the poem.
- Refer to and quote from the poem occasionally. Zone in on key words and phrases to support your point.
- Use paragraphs. If you are writing about more than one stanza, you could explore each stanza in a separate paragraph.
- Keep the answer focused on the question – the title 'Wounds'.
- Finish with a brief conclusion and restate your key point.

# My Poetry Revision Sheet
## Main Notes on Prescribed Poetry

Student's Name: _____ Date: _____

Subject: English, Paper 2, Section III, Poetry (Prescribed)

Poem Title: _____ Poet: _____

Reference page in textbook: _____ Date I revised these notes:_____

1. Write about the poem's title. (Is it a good one? Why? Could you suggest a different title? Give a reason why your title is an interesting one.)

2. Subject matter (write down briefly what the poem is about; does it tell a story, or describe a feeling?)

3. Theme of the poem (write down what the poet is saying about the poem's subject. What is the main message conveyed by the poem?)

4. Write briefly about each key section of the poem that 'shows' the theme clearly. (Use the phrase stanza for the different verses in the poem.)

Photocopy and use the table when revising your Prescribed Poems.

**5.** Write about the poet's use of language. (Identify any examples of imagery: similes, metaphors. If these are not used, give examples of any vivid, descriptive language. Write down why you think the poet used these words and phrases, why you think they are effective.)

**6.** Write down what effect the poem had on you. Explain why. (Did the poem make you feel sad, happy, or shocked? Try to focus on the key words/phrases/images that made you feel this way.)

**7.** What impression of the poet do you get from reading this poem. (Identify a key word first – the poet is a determined person; or the poet is an angry, caring, depressed or loving person. Then support your answer by referring to parts of the poem that give you that impression.)

**8.** Write down your favourite lines in the poem. Explain why you like them.

**9.** Overall, did you like or dislike this poem? Explain why.

# Key Exam Tips

## ⚙ Key Exam Tips and and Techniques for Poetry

- On your exam paper, write down your time allowance for this question beside the actual question.

- Read the question, at least twice. After your first reading, underline the key instructions.

- Then read the poem – not just quickly, but very closely. Look out for surprising words or unusual images. **Underline the key lines** in the poem that make an impact on you.

- Look back at the question once again. Once you understand clearly what the question is instructing you to do, you must plan your answer. This need only take a few minutes, but it is time very well spent.

- Read the title of the **Unseen Poem** carefully. If an introduction is provided, a glossary or some footnotes, take note of these as well. They might help you to understand the context of the poem: where, when, why it was written.

- Four **Prescribed Poems** will be printed on the exam paper.

- You must answer questions on one of these four poems.

- For your chosen poem, you must answer 1(i), 1(ii) and 1(iii).

- For Question 2, you answer *either* 2(i) or 2(ii) or 2(iii).

- Write about 10 lines to answer each part of Question 1. (1(i), 1(ii) and 1(iii) are worth 10 marks each.)

- Write about 20 lines to answer Question 2 (worth 20 marks).

- When writing your answer, remain focused on following the instructions. Do not drift off the point. Questions on prescribed poetry will ask you about the content of the poem (what it is about), but also about your own reading (interpretation) of the poem.

- Some questions may also ask you about the writer's use of language: vivid language, clear images, type of diction used, or evidence of rhyme patterns. Revise the glossary of poetic terms on Study Card No. 22 on page 220.

- Refer closely to the text of the poem in support of each answer that you write.

- Remember to use quotation marks (". . .") around the words, phrases or lines of poetry that you are quoting from the poem.

- Don't be afraid of making a personal response, but you must use the words and images from the poem to explain your viewpoint; doing this will earn you higher marks.

- If you can identify a simile or metaphor in a poem, you will get extra marks for pointing this out. But even more marks go for saying what effect a metaphor or simile has in the poem. Not all poems use imagery such as similes, but read the text carefully – if they are there, find them!

## ◉ Record of What I Have Learned Revising for Poetry

**Main Tips to Remember When Writing**

- **Answering the questions on an Unseen Poem**

  - _____
  - _____
  - _____
  - _____

- **Answering the questions on a Prescribed Poem**

  - _____
  - _____
  - _____
  - _____

Well done on completing this section! Keep up the good work and revise as many poems as you can. Use your revision sheets regularly – try to complete one each week. File them away in a ring binder for easy reference later.

**Date completed:**

# Your Last Minute Revision!

## ◉ Your Last Minute Revison Page!

### Around 5 Minutes Revision for Each Poetry Revision Sheet

● Revise your poetry revision sheets which you made out during the year. These should be in your own revision file.

### Around 10 Minutes Revision

● Revise your Study Card on Poetic Terms. You will find this on page 220.

### Around 10 Minutes Revision

● Read over the tips and techniques for answering on poetry in this chapter.

### Around 20 Minutes Revision

● It would be a good idea to remind yourself of the types of questions that have come up in previous years. Read the tips on answering these and the sample answers in this chapter.

### Around 5 Minutes Revision

### Check your Time Management

● **Paper 2, Section III, Poetry** (70 marks) overall time allowance = 65 minutes (includes reading time and planning time).

   ▪ **Unseen Poem** (20 marks) 15 minutes.

   ▪ **Prescribed Poem** (50 marks) 50 minutes.

# Poetry Revision Log

Name: _____

Poems I have revised for Leaving Certificate English, Year: 20____

| Poem | Poet | Page ref | Revision sheet completed | Date |
|------|------|----------|--------------------------|------|
|  |  |  |  |  |
|  |  |  |  |  |
|  |  |  |  |  |
|  |  |  |  |  |
|  |  |  |  |  |
|  |  |  |  |  |
|  |  |  |  |  |
|  |  |  |  |  |
|  |  |  |  |  |
|  |  |  |  |  |
|  |  |  |  |  |
|  |  |  |  |  |
|  |  |  |  |  |
|  |  |  |  |  |
|  |  |  |  |  |
|  |  |  |  |  |
|  |  |  |  |  |
|  |  |  |  |  |
|  |  |  |  |  |
|  |  |  |  |  |
|  |  |  |  |  |
|  |  |  |  |  |
|  |  |  |  |  |
|  |  |  |  |  |
|  |  |  |  |  |
|  |  |  |  |  |
|  |  |  |  |  |
|  |  |  |  |  |
|  |  |  |  |  |
|  |  |  |  |  |
|  |  |  |  |  |
|  |  |  |  |  |

# List of STUDY CARDS

**Notes**